Eyewitness
OLYMPICS

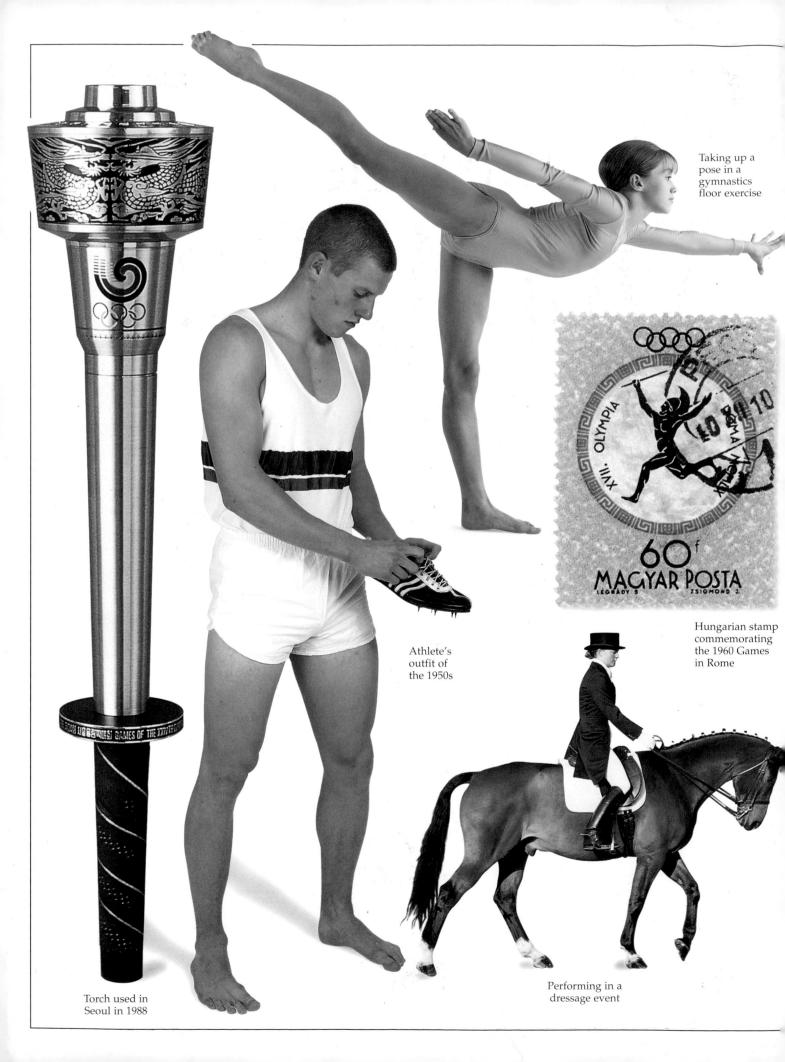

Taking up a
pose in a
gymnastics
floor exercise

60 f
MAGYAR POSTA

XVII. OLYMPIA

Hungarian stamp
commemorating
the 1960 Games
in Rome

Athlete's
outfit of
the 1950s

Torch used in
Seoul in 1988

Performing in a
dressage event

Wheelchair racing

Warming up
before training

Eyewitness
OLYMPICS

Written by
CHRIS OXLADE
& DAVID BALLHEIMER

Pin commemorating the
1924 Games in Paris

DK

LONDON, NEW YORK, MELBOURNE,
MUNICH, AND DELHI

Project editor Louise Pritchard
Art editor Jill Plank
Senior managing editor Linda Martin
Senior managing art editor Julia Harris
Production Kate Oliver
Picture researcher Sean Hunter
DTP designer Andrew O'Brien
Photographers Andy Crawford, Bob Langrish, Steve Teague

PAPERBACK EDITION
Managing editor Andrew Macintyre
Managing art editor Jane Thomas
Senior editor Kitty Blount
Editor and reference compiler Sarah Phillips
Art editor Andrew Nash
Production Jenny Jacoby
Picture research Carolyn Clerkin
DTP Designer Siu Yin Ho
Consultant Stan Greenberg

This Eyewitness ® Guide has been conceived by
Dorling Kindersley Limited and Editions Gallimard

Hardback edition first published in Great Britain in 1999
This edition published in Great Britain in 2004
by Dorling Kindersley Limited,
80 Strand, London WC2 0RL

2 4 6 8 10 9 7 5 3 1

Copyright © 1999, © 2004 Dorling Kindersley Limited, London
Penguin Group

A CIP catalogue record for this book is
available from the British Library.

ISBN 1 4053 0300 X

Colour reproduction by
Colourscan, Singapore
Printed in Singapore by Toppan, China

See our complete
catalogue at

www.dk.com

Commemorative
medal from the 1936
Games in Berlin

Starting blocks

Javelin shoe

Trainer

Sprint shoe

Swimming goggles

Exercising with
weights

Contents

Weight-lifting

What were the Olympics?

THE ORIGINS OF THE Olympic Games lie centuries ago in ancient Greece. They were part of a religious festival. Greek life revolved around religion, and sport was a way for the people to honour their gods. There were many local festivals but four national festivals called the Panhellenic Games were open to competitors from all Greek regions and colonies. These were the Pythian, the Nemean, the Isthmian, and the Olympic Games. They alternated so that there was a national athletic festival every year.

DELPHI STADIUM
Delphi was sacred to Apollo and the Greeks thought that it stood at the centre of the world. In the 5th century BC, they built this 7,000-seater athletics stadium on the hillside above the great Temple of Apollo. The spectators' stand and seats for supervisors can be seen among the ruins today.

HONOURING APOLLO
Different Games were celebrations to different gods and were held at or near religious sanctuaries. The Pythian Games were held in Delphi in honour of Apollo. The Isthmian Games in Corinth honoured Poseidon. Zeus was honoured at the Nemean Games in Nemea and at the Olympic Games in Olympia.

This ancient Greek vessel shows athletes racing in armour

Ancient Greek carving of Apollo

Laurel wreaths were awarded at the Pythian Games

Shield with runner's personal symbols on the outside

Fresh wild celery was awarded at the Nemean Games

Wreaths of olive leaves were awarded at the Olympic Games

Panathenaic amphora

RUNNER'S PRIZE
Winners at the Panathenaic Games in Athens were awarded an amphora, a two-handled vessel, full of finest olive oil. It was decorated with scenes of their particular event. This amphora shows racing in armour. Athletics and war were closely linked. Competing in sports was a way of keeping fit for battle.

Athlete wearing a helmet and carrying a shield as he races

FLORAL TRIBUTES
At the Panhellenic Games, floral tributes were given to the winners. Most prized of all was an Olympic olive wreath, cut from a sacred tree that stood behind Zeus's temple at Olympia. Originally, all the athletes were amateurs but eventually, at all but the Olympic Games, they received prize-money and even appearance-money.

Wreaths of pine branches were awarded at the Isthmian Games

The javelin was a powerful weapon, but sporting javelins were lighter than those used in battle. Ancient Greek athletes held their javelin by a leather thong knotted or twisted around the shaft. When the javelin was released, the thong unwound, making the javelin spin as it flew through the air.

Greek vase painting

The sporting javelin was made of elder

Most discuses used in the Games were made of bronze and were heavier than the modern version

ATHLETES AND EVENTS

This famous figure of a young man throwing a discus is a Roman copy of a statue originally created in bronze in about 450 BC, probably by the Greek sculptor Myron. Throwing the discus was one of the five disciplines in the pentathlon. The others were running, jumping, throwing the javelin, and wrestling. Other events held at the Games were boxing, chariot racing, and horse racing.

Greek artists took care to depict the muscles and strength of an athlete

Roman copy of a statue called The Discobolus, made in the 1st century AD

Long hair held back in a band

Bare right shoulder

Statuette was made in about 500 BC

Athletes competed nude in most events. One legend says that this was because an athlete once lost his loincloth during a race, and everyone realized it would be easier to compete with nothing on

This athlete is poised, ready to launch his discus

A tunic reaches to just above the girl's knee

Bronze statuette of a girl runner from Sparta

WOMEN AT THE GAMES

As a rule, women were not allowed to compete at the Games until the 2nd century AD. They were never allowed at the Olympic Games, even as spectators. There was a separate women's festival at Olympia called the Heraia, held every four years in honour of the goddess Hera, wife of Zeus. The only sporting event at the Heraia was a short race. The situation was different in Sparta, a state in southern ancient Greece. Here, girls were encouraged to take part in sport and games to make them strong so that they would later produce good Spartan soldiers.

The ancient Games

VICTORY
The winged figure on this cast of a stone seal represents Nike, or Victory. She is crowning an athlete with an olive wreath. Winning was everything at the Olympics. Losers were quickly forgotten.

THE FIRST RECORD of the Olympic Games dates from 776 BC, but they were probably established hundreds of years before that. The Olympics began as a small event but gradually gained popularity to become the premier festival in Greece. For at least 1,000 years, they were held every four years, and survived in spite of numerous wars and the Roman invasion of Greece in about AD 150. The Games became so important that the Greeks recorded historical events according to the Olympiad, or four-year period, in which they took place.

MUSIC AND DANCE
The religious ceremonies and sporting events at Olympia were part of a greater festival. Tens of thousands of spectators flocked there to watch the Games and visit the temples. They were kept well entertained by singers, dancers, conjurers, public speakers, and poets. Food and flower sellers, pedlars, and bookmakers set up their tents and stalls outside the sacred site.

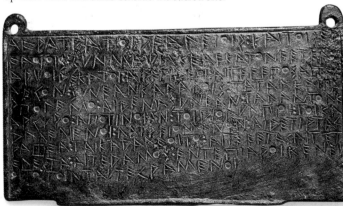

THE OLYMPIC TRUCE
Ancient Greece was not a single country but a collection of independent city-states that were often at war with each other. During the Olympic Games, an agreement called the Sacred Truce declared that all hostilities must cease for a month. The Truce was backed by peace treaties, such as the one shown on this tablet between the state of Elis, containing Olympia, and a neighbouring state.

IN HONOUR OF ZEUS
The Olympic Games were held in honour of Zeus. On the third day of the Games, a procession of competitors, judges, and important guests made its way to the Altar of Zeus, to sacrifice 100 oxen. The most important building at Olympia was the great Temple of Zeus. Inside stood a statue of the god, 13 m (43 ft) tall, cast in gold and ivory. It was one of the seven wonders of the ancient world. At the end of the 4th century, the statue was taken to a palace In Constantinople (now Istanbul), where it was later destroyed in a fire.

Zeus is said to have hurled a thunderbolt and claimed the spot where it landed in Olympia as his sacred precinct

Zeus is usually depicted as strong, bearded, and middle-aged

Roman statuette of Zeus from 2nd century BC

Gymnasium, where runners and throwers trained

Palaistra, for jumping and combat training

The Temple of Hera, the first temple on the site

Treasuries, where valuables were stored

Stadium – 192 m (630 ft) long and 32 m (105 ft) wide

OLYMPIA

This remote religious sanctuary was about 50 km (31 miles) from the city of Elis. There was no town or city at Olympia. When the Olympics began in the 8th century BC, the site consisted of a sacred area but no buildings. Over the next 1,000 years, many buildings were constructed, including temples, altars, colonnades, and sports arenas. This model of Olympia shows the site as it would have looked in about 100 BC.

Probable site of the hippodrome, where chariot and horse racing took place

Open-air swimming pool with steps leading down from each side

Leonidaion, a hotel for visiting officials

Sacred olive tree

Temple of Zeus

Southern colonnade from which spectators could watch the chariots going to the hippodrome

Starting gates of the hippodrome

Heracles supporting the world on his shoulders for Atlas

The goddess Athena assisting Heracles

Section of a frieze from the Temple of Zeus at Olympia

THE PALAISTRA AT OLYMPIA

These columns are the remains of the palaistra at Olympia, where athletes trained for jumping and combat events. The palaistra was a low building around a central courtyard. It contained dressing rooms, baths, and a washroom. Every Greek city had its own palaistra.

Boxers wrapped leather thongs around their hands over a sheepskin lining

Boxing contests could last for several hours

HERACLES

According to myth, Olympia was created by the greatest Greek hero of them all, Heracles, son of Zeus. Heracles is famous for performing 12 seemingly impossible tasks, or labours. He started the Olympic Games in honour of Zeus to celebrate the completion of one of these tasks – the cleaning of the cattle stables of King Augeas of Elis.

OLYMPIC EVENTS

There were no team events at the ancient Olympics. To begin with, the only event was a short foot-race – about 200 m (656 ft). Boxing and other sports were gradually added. Legend has it that Apollo beat Ares, the god of war, in the first boxing match at Olympia.

Boxing scene from an amphora given as a prize in about 336 BC

Olympia discovered

AFTER AD 261, THERE ARE no further records of Olympic winners, so we do not know for certain when the ancient Games came to an end. When Rome made Greece part of its empire, the Games began to decline. In AD 393, the Christian emperor Theodosius I decreed that all pagan centres be closed down, and Olympia was eventually abandoned. A succession of invaders destroyed the site, and any remaining buildings were ruined by earthquakes and fire. Flooding from nearby rivers finally covered the ruins with several metres of mud and it was 1,000 years before Olympia's buildings were seen again.

END OF THE GAMES
A portrait of the Roman emperor Theodosius II appears on this ancient gold coin. In AD 426, Theodosius II had the Temple of Zeus and other buildings at Olympia burned down. This may have been when the Olympic Games finally came to an end.

ERNST CURTIUS
Archaeologists began the search for Olympia in the 18th century, but the most important excavations were carried out between 1875 and 1891 by the German Archaeological Institute. Directed by Professor Ernst Curtius, a team unearthed the remains of almost all the buildings. They found 130 statues and more than 6,000 clay, gold, and bronze objects.

Ernst Curtius in about 1880

MODERN-DAY EXCAVATIONS
Most of Olympia had been explored by the end of the 19th century, but excavations have continued on a smaller scale up to the present day. For example, between 1958 and 1961, a German team finished excavating the stadium and rebuilt the banked spectator area.

RUINED GYMNASIUM
The German archaeologists did not find any buildings still standing at Olympia, but they reconstructed many of the toppled remains. This view shows part of the huge gymnasium complex, where athletes trained under cover. It was large enough to contain a running track the same length as the main stadium.

STATUE OF NIKE
This statue of Nike, or Victory, descending from the heavens remarkably survived almost in one piece. Made in 425 BC by Paionios of Mende, the statue is 3 m (9.8 ft) high. It stood on the top of a column, a further 9 m (29.5 ft) tall, in front of the Temple of Zeus.

Nike's face may have been destroyed by Christians in the time of Theodosius II

Remains of wings

Nike's clothes were originally painted red

BRONZE GODDESS

Archaeologists have found hundreds of statuettes and figurines, mostly of bronze, like this goddess, or of terracotta. There are gods, heroes, warriors, runners, animals, and chariots complete with charioteers. The figures were offered to the gods by athletes and spectators.

Most statues at Olympia were paid for by winning athletes and dedicated to Zeus

Long nose-piece and cheek guards are typical of a Corinthian helmet

Bronze statue of a goddess from 520 BC

SPOILS OF WAR

Ancient Greek warriors gave arms and armour captured in battle as offerings to the gods. Shields, breast plates, helmets, arrow heads, spears, and other weapons have all been found at Olympia. This bronze helmet carries an inscription that says that it was dedicated to Zeus as spoil taken from the Corinthians.

Zeus carries off Ganymede

The boxer's face is covered in scars

This bronze head is 28 cm (11 in) high

CUTS AND BRUISES

This bronze head, found at Olympia in 1880, is a portrait of a boxer called Satyros. Boxing in ancient times was an even tougher sport than boxing today. There were no rounds, to give the boxers a break, and no time limit. The sculptor gave this boxer wounds to make him look realistic.

ZEUS SEIZES GANYMEDE

Some finds at Olympia are amazingly well preserved. This terracotta statue of Zeus and Ganymede was found in the stadium area. It was made in 470 BC, possibly by a famous sculptor called Pheidias who made many of the statues at Olympia in his workshop near the gymnasium. In Greek legend, Zeus carried off Ganymede to be his cup-bearer because of his beauty.

The Olympics reborn

MORE THAN 1,500 YEARS after the ancient Greek Olympic Games came to an end, the Frenchman Baron Pierre de Coubertin had a dream to bring the Games back to life. At a conference on international sport, held in Paris in 1894, Coubertin put forward a resolution to revive the Games. His idea was enthusiastically received and the International Olympic Committee (IOC) was founded, with Coubertin among its members. Just two years later, in Athens in April 1896, the king of Greece declared open the first Olympic Games of the modern era. Over the next 100 years, the Olympics gradually grew into the fabulous sporting occasion we know today.

Carving of Zeus

BURIED HEART
At Olympia, the Greeks raised a monument to Pierre de Coubertin to thank him for his efforts in reviving the Olympics. Coubertin's last wish was that his heart should be kept for ever at Olympia. It is buried beneath the monument.

Inscription honours Coubertin's work in reviving the Olympic Games

Coubertin won a gold medal for poetry at the Stockholm Games in 1912

Founding father

Without Baron Pierre de Coubertin, it is unlikely that the modern Olympic Games would exist. Coubertin believed that sport was vital for the mental as well as the physical development of young people, and that international sporting competition would help people from different nations to become friends. Coubertin himself was a keen sportsman, although not an outstanding one.

MEMORIAL BADGE
This memorial medal was struck "to the reviver of the Olympic Games". Coubertin was fascinated by ancient Greece. His dream of a modern Olympics was boosted when archaeologists discovered the ruins of Olympia in 1875.

PIERRE DE COUBERTIN
Pierre de Coubertin was born in Paris, France, on New Year's Day 1863. He was president of the International Olympic Committee from 1896 to 1925 and was awarded the Nobel Peace Prize in 1920. He died in Geneva, Switzerland, in 1937.

BIRTH OF THE RINGS
On a visit to Delphi, site of the ancient Pythian Games, Pierre de Coubertin saw the emblem of five linked rings on this altar. It gave him the idea for the design on the Olympic flag. The five intertwined rings symbolized the five continents of the world that participated in the Games: Africa, Asia, America, Europe, and Australasia.

Wreath of olive leaves laid in remembrance

The five-ring symbol on this ancient Greek altar at Delphi represented five circles on a sacred discus, in which the terms of the truce for the Pythian Games were inscribed

THE FIRST STADIUM
The Panathenean Stadium in Athens was specially built for the 1896 Olympic Games. It was a marble replica of an ancient stadium originally built in 330 BC, and was built on the same site. The arena was long and narrow, and runners in the longer races had to slow down to negotiate the tight bends at each end of the track.

JUST THE TICKET
A ticket for the Olympic Games in 1896 cost two drachmas. More than 60,000 spectators turned up for the opening day. The competitors were not the world's best athletes because anybody could take part. Most competitors were Greek; some were tourists who entered at the last minute.

POSTERS AND POSTAGE
The design for this poster (left) for the 1896 Games has a classical feel, showing the ancient buildings of the Acropolis. The Games had no official sponsors, although the Greek royal family offered some financial support. Special postage stamps and a lottery also helped to fund the Games.

896
winner's
medal

Greek lettering denoting the Olympic Games

Image of the Acropolis in Athens

A winner's medal in 1896 was silver, not gold

MARATHON STARTS
One of the races in 1896 was run from the plains of Marathon, north of Athens, to the new stadium. It was run in honour of Pheidippides, a legendary warrior who, after the Battle of Marathon in 490 BC, ran from the battlefield with news of the victory of the Athenians over the Persians. He then dropped dead. The 1896 marathon was appropriately won by a Greek runner, Spiridon Louis, seen here in national dress.

FIRST MEDALS WON
Coubertin thought that the awarding of medals would be an incentive to athletes to take part in the Olympics. Winners in Athens in 1896 were presented with a silver medal, an olive branch, and a certificate; runners-up received a copper medal and a sprig of laurel.

Traditions

ANCIENT TRADITIONS

This inside of a cup, shows a boxer at prayer. At the ancient Olympics, whole days were given over to religious ceremonies.

"IN THE NAME OF all the competitors, I promise that we shall take part in these Olympic Games, respecting and abiding by the rules which govern them, in the true spirit of sportsmanship, for the glory of sport, and the honour of our teams." So goes the Olympic oath, spoken by one athlete at the opening ceremony of every Olympic Games. It reminds us of the Olympic tradition that competition must be fair and friendly, and that taking part is more important than winning. All the Olympic ceremonies and symbols reflect the aim of the Olympic movement to promote understanding between the nations of the world.

TORCH RELAY

As a symbol of international unity, the Olympic flame is taken by torch relay across national borders from the ancient site of Olympia to the Olympic venue. Where possible, it is taken by runners, who run 1 km (1,094 yd) each. Sometimes it goes by boat or plane. The flame is transferred from torch to torch. When it reaches the stadium, it is taken around the track and then used to ignite the main flame that burns throughout the Games.

LIGHTING THE FLAME

The Olympic flame is lit at the altar of the goddess Hera at Olympia, where a flame burned during the ancient Olympic Games. A torch is lit using a concave mirror to concentrate light from the Sun. Before the flame begins its journey to the Olympic stadium, it is used to light a flame in the Coubertin Grove in honour of Pierre de Coubertin.

Unusual openwork design

1,688 torches were used in the 1948 relay. This is the torch used by the last runner at the opening ceremony

1936 torch was modelled on those seen on ancient artefacts

1936 – Berlin, Germany. This was the first time the flame was lit at Olympia and taken by torch relay. It went via Athens and covered 3,075 km (1,910 miles).

1948 – London, UK. The torch relay was diverted to go past Coubertin's tomb.

Fluted handle

Olympic rings and wreath

Only 22 torches were made, so, for the first time, the runners did not each have their own torch

1952 – Helsinki, Finland. To the delight of the crowd, Paavo Nurmi carried the torch into the Olympic stadium and passed it to Hannes Kolehmainen at the foot of the stadium tower.

16

Poster advertising the 1928 Olympic Games

Opening ceremony, Nagano, Japan, 1998

FIRST LIGHT

The Olympic flame was first lit at the 1928 Olympic Games in Amsterdam. It burned throughout the Games in the stadium at the top of a tower that was 50 m (164 ft) high.

OPENING CEREMONY

A spectacular display now always forms part of the opening ceremony at the Olympic Games. After the display, the competitors enter the stadium. The Greek team always leads the parade, and the host team always enters last. One of the athletes and one of the judges take the Olympic oath of fair play on behalf of the others. At the closing ceremony, the president of the International Olympic Committee calls for the youth of the world to gather again in four years' time.

Gold-plated upper part

1952 – Oslo, Norway. The torch relay for the winter Games started at the historic Norwegian town of Morgedal.

1960 – Squaw Valley, USA. The main flame for these winter Games was lit from this torch by the 1952 speed-skating champion Kenneth Henry.

1968 – Mexico City, Mexico. Enriqueta Basilio became the first woman to light the flame.

Silver-plated handle

1980 – Moscow, USSR. Sergei Belov and Victor Saneyev were the last runners.

Leather handle with a metallic ring

1992 – Albertville, France. The flame was lit by the French soccer star Michel Platini and a local child.

Dove design on the poster for the Moscow Games of 1980

DOVES OF PEACE

During the opening ceremony, hundreds of doves are released into the air from cages in the stadium as a symbol of peace. Doves of peace were released at the very first modern Olympic Games in 1896.

1984 – Los Angeles, USA. The granddaughter of Jesse Owens carried the torch on the last leg, and also on the first leg with the grandson of the great Olympian Jim Thorpe.

OLYMPIC FLAG

The Olympic flag has flown at the Games since 1920. It was designed to include at least one colour in the flag of every country. At the closing ceremony, the flag is given to a representative of the hosts of the next Games.

From the beginning

THE OLYMPIC GAMES are held in the first year of each four-year Olympiad. Athens 1896 was in the I Olympiad; Athens 2004 will be the Games of the XXVIII (28th) Olympiad. They will be in fact only the 25th summer Olympic Games because the Games of three Olympiads were not held due to war. The first winter Olympic Games were held in 1924 in the VIII (8th) Olympiad. There was little interest in the summer Games of 1900 and 1904, so, in 1906, a 10th-anniversary Games were held in Athens. These are known as the Interim or Intercalated Games.

BRONZE MEDAL
This medal, struck to commemorate the first modern Olympic Games in Athens, shows the goddess Athena holding an olive wreath.

OLYMPIC SOUVENIR
Many different souvenirs have been made for the Olympic Games. This is a clothing pin commemorating the Paris Games of 1900.

THE GREAT STADIUM SHEPHERD'S BUSH LONDON

THE OLYMPIC GAMES 1908 PROGRAMME 6d

LONDON 1908
London had less than two years to prepare for the 1908 Olympics, but the Games were still the best organized so far.

Programme cover for the 1908 Games

1896	1900	1904	1908	1912	1920
ATHENS, GREECE All 300 competitors at the first modern Games were men. American students took the athletics by storm, although they did not arrive until the eve of the Games because of a mix-up with dates. Among them was the first Olympic champion, triple-jumper James Connolly. The cricket and soccer events were cancelled due to lack of entrants.	**PARIS, FRANCE** Held as part of the Paris International Exhibition, the Games became a sideshow to the main event. They were spread over five months and there was little interest from the public. The facilities were sub-standard and the swimming was held in the river Seine. Ray Ewry (USA) won the standing high, long, and triple jumps.	**ST LOUIS, USA** As in Paris, the St Louis Games were part of a trade fair. Events for schoolboys were included that were not Olympic sports. There were far fewer athletes than in 1900 because of the difficulty of travelling from Europe. Non-Americans won only two athletics events – an Irishman won the decathlon, and a Canadian won the 56-lb weight throw.	**LONDON, UK** The Games should have been held in Rome, but the Italian government had to divert funds to help the victims of the eruption of Mount Vesuvius in 1906. The lasting image is of marathon runner Dorando Pietri being helped over the line in first place. He was disqualified but was later given a special gold cup by Queen Alexandra.	**STOCKHOLM, SWEDEN** The 1912 Games were the most efficient so far. Among the new events were women's swimming and the modern pentathlon, devised by Pierre de Coubertin as a test of the all-round sportsman. Hannes Kolehmainen, the first of the "flying Finns", took gold in the 5000 m, 10,000 m, and the cross-country.	**ANTWERP, BELGIUM** The first Games after the First World War saw the Olympic flag flying for the first time. The Olympic oath was also heard for the first time. Germany, Bulgaria, Hungary, and Turkey were not invited because of their part in starting the war. On the track, Finnish distance runner Paavo Nurmi made his mark.

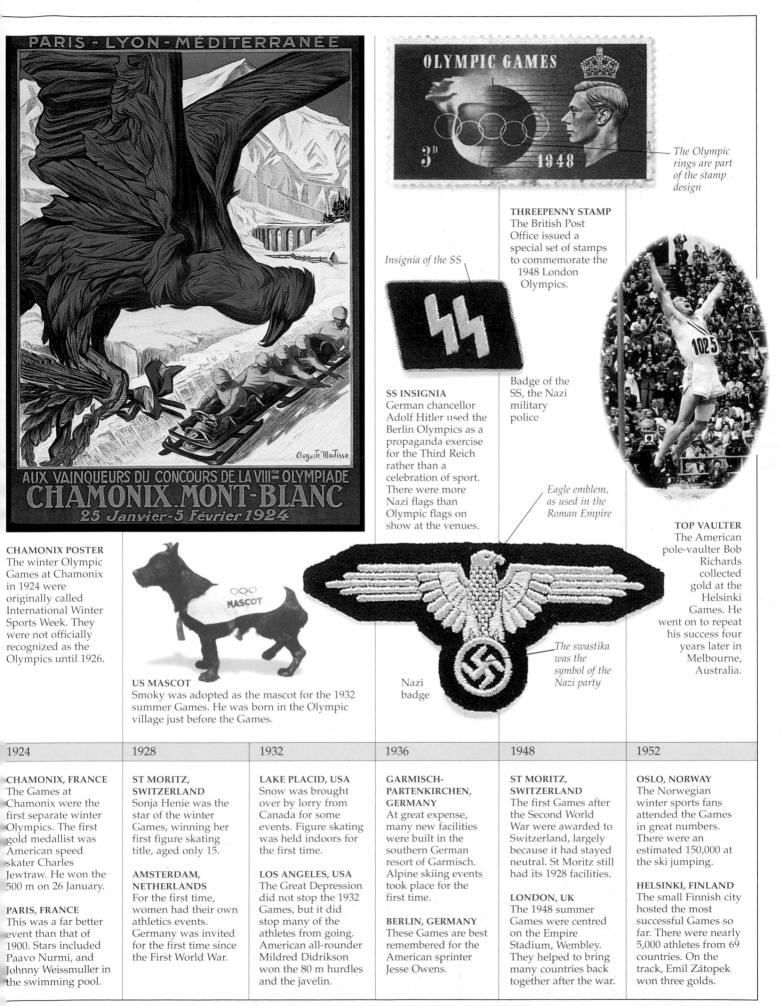

PARIS · LYON · MÉDITERRANÉE

AUX VAINQUEURS DU CONCOURS DE LA VIIIᵐᵉ OLYMPIADE
CHAMONIX · MONT-BLANC
25 Janvier–5 Février 1924

Auguste Matisse

CHAMONIX POSTER
The winter Olympic Games at Chamonix in 1924 were originally called International Winter Sports Week. They were not officially recognized as the Olympics until 1926.

MASCOT

US MASCOT
Smoky was adopted as the mascot for the 1932 summer Games. He was born in the Olympic village just before the Games.

OLYMPIC GAMES 3ᴰ 1948

The Olympic rings are part of the stamp design

THREEPENNY STAMP
The British Post Office issued a special set of stamps to commemorate the 1948 London Olympics.

Insignia of the SS

SS INSIGNIA
German chancellor Adolf Hitler used the Berlin Olympics as a propaganda exercise for the Third Reich rather than a celebration of sport. There were more Nazi flags than Olympic flags on show at the venues.

Badge of the SS, the Nazi military police

Eagle emblem, as used in the Roman Empire

Nazi badge

The swastika was the symbol of the Nazi party

102 5

TOP VAULTER
The American pole-vaulter Bob Richards collected gold at the Helsinki Games. He went on to repeat his success four years later in Melbourne, Australia.

1924	1928	1932	1936	1948	1952
CHAMONIX, FRANCE The Games at Chamonix were the first separate winter Olympics. The first gold medallist was American speed skater Charles Jewtraw. He won the 500 m on 26 January. **PARIS, FRANCE** This was a far better event than that of 1900. Stars included Paavo Nurmi, and Johnny Weissmuller in the swimming pool.	**ST MORITZ, SWITZERLAND** Sonja Henie was the star of the winter Games, winning her first figure skating title, aged only 15. **AMSTERDAM, NETHERLANDS** For the first time, women had their own athletics events. Germany was invited for the first time since the First World War.	**LAKE PLACID, USA** Snow was brought over by lorry from Canada for some events. Figure skating was held indoors for the first time. **LOS ANGELES, USA** The Great Depression did not stop the 1932 Games, but it did stop many of the athletes from going. American all-rounder Mildred Didrikson won the 80 m hurdles and the javelin.	**GARMISCH-PARTENKIRCHEN, GERMANY** At great expense, many new facilities were built in the southern German resort of Garmisch. Alpine skiing events took place for the first time. **BERLIN, GERMANY** These Games are best remembered for the American sprinter Jesse Owens.	**ST MORITZ, SWITZERLAND** The first Games after the Second World War were awarded to Switzerland, largely because it had stayed neutral. St Moritz still had its 1928 facilities. **LONDON, UK** The 1948 summer Games were centred on the Empire Stadium, Wembley. They helped to bring many countries back together after the war.	**OSLO, NORWAY** The Norwegian winter sports fans attended the Games in great numbers. There were an estimated 150,000 at the ski jumping. **HELSINKI, FINLAND** The small Finnish city hosted the most successful Games so far. There were nearly 5,000 athletes from 69 countries. On the track, Emil Zátopek won three golds.

Continued on next page

1956–2002

The second half of the 20th century saw changes in the Olympics. From the 1960s, television coverage turned them into a global event. This attracted commercial sponsors, who now help to pay for the Games in return for the advertising they receive. A previous ban on professionals has been lifted, although most competitors are still amateurs. The winter Games have moved to a new four-year cycle, two years out of step with the summer Games.

Karl Schranz lost out in 1968 too. He was allowed rerun after a person crossed his path. He then had the fastest time, but was later disqualified for missing two gates before he had been distracted in his first run

CORTINA 1956
Commercial sponsors helped the northern Italian town to build new venues for the winter Games. There were Soviet competitors at the winter Games for the first time.

Design for the 1956 winter Olympics

PRO OUT
Austrian skier Karl Schranz was banned on the day before the Sapporo Games began for accepting sponsorship money, and therefore not being a true amateur. Thirty-nine other athletes were in the same position, but Schranz was the only one to be banned.

BOYCOTTS
After a New Zealand rugby tour of apartheid-governed South Africa, 24 teams boycotted the Montreal Games. They objected to New Zealand being there.

FOSBURY FLOP
In 1968, Dick Fosbury won high-jump gold for the USA by clearing the bar shoulders first rather than by straddling it. This new style was adopted by most high jumpers and became known as the Fosbury flop.

1956	1960	1964	1968	1972	1976
CORTINA, ITALY The USSR dominated the ice hockey. The Austrian Toni Sailer won gold in all three Alpine titles. **MELBOURNE, AUSTRALIA** The summer Games were the first held outside Europe or the USA. Quarantine rules prevented horses from entering the country, so the equestrian events were held in Sweden.	**SQUAW VALLEY, USA** A resort was specially built for the winter Games. The opening ceremony was devised by Walt Disney. **ROME, ITALY** The Games were broadcast live on TV to millions in Europe. Cassius Clay (now Muhammad Ali) won gold in the boxing. Abebe Bikila won the marathon barefoot. The first Paralympics took place afterwards.	**INNSBRUCK, AUSTRIA** Poor weather in the resort meant that thousands of tonnes of snow had to be brought to the pistes. **TOKYO, JAPAN** The Japanese spared no expense, building a new road system around Tokyo. The flame was lit by a student who was born near Hiroshima in 1945 on the day the atomic bomb fell.	**GRENOBLE, FRANCE** Venues for the winter Games were spread around the region. Frenchman Jean-Claude Killy won all the Alpine events. **MEXICO CITY, MEXICO** The high altitude meant that distance runners struggled to breathe in the thin air. It helped long jumper Bob Beamon to a world record, which lasted until 1991.	**SAPPORO, JAPAN** The huge sums given by TV companies for rights to the winter Games paid for the fabulous facilities in the Japanese city. **MUNICH, GERMANY** Seventeen people died in a terrorist attack on the Israeli team. In the Games, US swimmer Mark Spitz won seven gold medals and Soviet gymnast Olga Korbut won three.	**INNSBRUCK, AUSTRIA** The winter Games were transferred from Denver, USA, because of spiralling costs. German skier Rosi Mittermaier won two golds and a silver. **MONTREAL, CANADA** There was extra security at the Games because of the events of 1972. On the track, Lasse Virén repeated his 1972 5000 m and 10,000 m double.

A "human torch" was part of the elaborate display in Moscow

Costume reflects the American flag

1980 OPENING
More than 100,000 spectators watched the opening ceremony in the Lenin Stadium in Moscow. Some teams protested against the Soviets by marching under the Olympic flag rather than their countries' flags.

The eagle is an emblem of the USA

SAM THE EAGLE
The mascot for the 1984 Los Angeles Games was the stars-and-stripes-clad Sam the Eagle.

Sydney 2000 TM©

DRUG SHAME
At Seoul, in the Olympics' worst drug scandal, Canadian Ben Johnson failed a drug test. He was stripped of his medal three days after winning the 100 m in a world-record time.

SYDNEY LOGO
In 1993, Australia's largest city, Sydney, was awarded the 2000 Olympic Games, dubbed the Millennium Games. More than 10,000 competitors took part and over 46,000 volunteers helped to make these Games a great success.

1980	1984	1988	1992/1994	1996/1998	2000/2002
LAKE PLACID, USA Artificial snow made its winter Olympics debut at Lake Placid. American speed skater Eric Heiden won five golds. **MOSCOW, USSR** Many countries boycotted the Games because of the Soviet invasion of Afghanistan. The battle between the British athletes Coe and Ovett ended with one gold each.	**SARAJEVO, YUGOSLAVIA** Stars of the winter Games were British ice dancers Torvill and Dean. Winter Paralympics were held for the first time. **LOS ANGELES, USA** The Games returned to the stadium of 1932. There was a Soviet boycott, but the Games are better remembered for the performances of American Carl Lewis.	**CALGARY, CANADA** The most successful competitor was the Finnish ski-jumper Matti Nykänen, who won three golds. **SEOUL, KOREA** There were no major boycotts, and athletes from 159 countries took part. On the track, Florence Griffith-Joyner won four sprint medals. Kristin Otto of East Germany swam to six golds.	**ALBERTVILLE, FRANCE** There were new sports in the winter Games including freestyle skiing. **BARCELONA, SPAIN** Athletes of the old USSR entered as the Unified Team. South Africa returned, plus a reunited Germany. **LILLEHAMMER, NORWAY** In 1994, the new four-year cycle of winter Games began.	**ATLANTA, USA** In 1996, Atlanta held the centenary Games. Not even a bomb, which killed two people in the Centennial Olympic Park, could spoil the party. Michael Johnson completed the first-ever 200 m and 400 m double. **NAGANO, JAPAN** Curling, women's ice hockey, and snowboarding made their debut.	**SYDNEY, AUSTRALIA** Two new sports introduced at these Games were the triathlon and taekwondo. Marion Jones (USA) won five medals in athletics. **SALT LAKE CITY, USA** The skeleton was reinstated and women's bobsled introduced. Alpine skier Janica Kostelic (Croatia) won three gold medals and one silver medal.

The summer Games

COMPETITORS AT THE SYDNEY Olympic Games in 2000 took part in a total of 28 different sports and groups of sports. Within these sports were 300 individual and team events in which medals were won. Some team events, such as the athletic relays, are separate from the individual events; others, such as the equestrian sport of show-jumping, are decided by combining the results of a country's individual representatives. Two Olympic events are made up of a combination of different sports. They are the modern pentathlon, consisting of épée fencing, swimming, pistol shooting, running, and riding, and the triathlon, consisting of running, swimming, and cycling. The triathlon was included at the Olympic Games for the first time in Sydney.

HURDLING
There are two sprint hurdling events – 100 m for women (110 m for men, shown here by British athlete Colin Jackson) over 10 hurdles, and the 400 m over 10 slightly lower hurdles. Men also run the 3000 m steeplechase, over 28 hurdles and seven water jumps.

Athletics
Most of the events in track and field athletics fall into three categories – running events, throwing events, and jumping events. Other events are walking and the combined events of the 10-discipline decathlon for men and the 7-discipline heptathlon for women.

Men's javelins are 2.7 m (8.8 ft) long; women's are 2.3 m (7.5 ft) long

JAVELIN
The javelin is one of the four Olympic throwing events. This drawing shows the 1908 and 1912 gold medalist Eric Lemming of Sweden. The other throwing events are the shot put, discus, and hammer. In each event, the competitor who throws the furthest wins gold.

Sprinters use starting blocks

Footplates can be adjusted to suit the athlete

RUNNING
Running events without hurdles can be divided into sprints (100, 200, and 400 m), middle-distance (800 and 1500 m), and long-distance (5000 m and 10,000 m and the marathon). Teams of four compete in relays at 4 x 100 m and 4 x 400 m, traditionally the last event of the track and field programme.

JUMPING
The jumping events are long jump (shown here by Jackie Joyner-Kersee of the USA), high jump, triple jump, and pole vault. Long-jump and triple-jump athletes have six attempts. High-jump and pole-vault athletes have three attempts at each height.

Ribbon flows through the air, following the gymnast's arm movements

A short stick is attached to the ribbon

WATER SPORTS

Canoeing (shown here by Germans Berro and Trummer in the 1992 Olympic C2 final), kayaking, sailing, and rowing are the Olympic water sports. In canoeing (with single-blade paddles) and kayaking (with double-blade paddles), there are flat-water sprints and white-water slaloms.

Balletic movements are part of rhythmic gymnastics

The ribbon must be kept moving

TARGET SPORTS

Archery, as shown here, and shooting are the Olympic target sports. Archers shoot over four distances and combine the scores. There are 15 shooting events in which competitors fire at stationary targets with rifles and pistols or at clay pigeons with shotguns.

Rhythmic gymnasts perform to music while using hand apparatus

GYMNASTICS

Artistic gymnastics consists of six disciplines for men (floor, pommel horse, rings, vault, parallel bars, and horizontal bar) and four disciplines for women (vault, uneven bars, balance beam, and floor). The separate events of trampolining and the ballet-like rhythmic gymnastics for women are also part of the gymnastics programme.

Items of rhythmic gymnastics apparatus

Spanish road cyclist Miguel Indurain at the 1996 Olympics

Clubs

Rope

Rhythmic gymnasts perform on the floor only

Hoops

CYCLING

Olympic cycling is divided into track cycling on an oval, banked track, road racing, and mountain biking. Track and road events include ordinary races, time trials against the clock, and pursuits, in which one cyclist or team attempts to catch another.

Continued on next page

Weights are colour-coded:
red = 25 kg (55 lb)
yellow = 15 kg (33 lb)

Dressage riders
dress formally for
competition

EQUESTRIAN SPORTS

Riding has been part of the modern Games since 1912. There are three events – show-jumping, dressage, and the three-day event. The last of these is made up of dressage, cross-country, and show-jumping sections, held on separate days. In each event, there are individual and team golds to be won.

Weights are made
of rubber with
metal plates inside

Lifters are
divided into 10
weight classes

WEIGHT-LIFTING

There are two lifts in weight-lifting events at the Olympic Games. In the clean and jerk, the bar is lifted in two movements, first to the shoulders and then above the head. In the snatch, the bar is lifted above the head in one movement.

The horse must
show obedience,
flexibility, and
athletic power

In halt, the
horse stands
still and
square

COMBAT SPORTS

Olympic combat sports are judo (shown here by Kenzo Nakamura and Martin Schmidt in 1996), taekwondo, boxing, wrestling, and fencing. There are three types of fencing – foil, épée, and sabre. In the other sports, athletes are divided into weight categories. There are two wrestling styles – Greco-Roman and freestyle.

In Olympic dressage,
the horse is asked to
perform only natural
movements

RACQUET AND BAT SPORTS
Table tennis and badminton have been added to the Olympic programme since 1988, and tennis has been reinstated. In each event, men and women can win medals for singles and doubles. Only badminton has a mixed-doubles event. Tennis is one of the few Olympic sports in which world-famous professionals are seen in action.

Most tennis racquets are strung with synthetic strings

AQUATICS
Swimming (shown here by Australian Shane Gould in 1972), diving, synchronized swimming, and water polo take place in the 50-m (164-ft) pool. There are 16 events in both the men's and women's swimming programmes, including relays. Diving is divided into 3 m springboard and 10 m platform events.

Tennis was not included at the Olympics for many years because of the amateurs-only rule

Team sports

The Olympic team sports are basketball, soccer, volleyball, hockey (properly called field hockey), handball, baseball (for men only), and softball (for women only). Water polo is a team sport played in the pool. Many famous professionals compete in the team sports at the Olympics, now that restrictions on professional athletes have been lifted.

SOCCER
Olympic soccer is not as important as the World Cup, and many nations do not compete. All but three players in a men's team must be under 23, but there are no age restrictions for the women's event. This action is from the 1996 women's semi-final between Brazil and China.

Basketball signed by the 1992 US "Dream Team"

The 1992 "Dream Team" won each of their games by an average of 44 points

VOLLEYBALL
Standard volleyball is played indoors, with teams of six. The ball must not touch the ground, and players send it over the high net with their hands. This picture shows the Netherlands v Italy in 1996. Beach volleyball, with two players per side, was introduced to the Olympics in Atlanta 1996.

HOCKEY
Field hockey is an 11-a-side team game in which the ball is passed and shot with a stick. Goals are scored in a similar way to soccer. No contact is allowed between the players. Olympic hockey tournaments are now played on an artificial pitch. The women's match shown here is Australia v Spain in 1996.

BASKETBALL
There are men's and women's basketball events. Olympic basketball includes one of the closest games in history. In the 1972 final, the USSR broke the USA's six-times gold-winning streak with a 51-50 win. Professionals were allowed into the 1992 Games, and the basketball was won by the USA's 'Dream Team' made up of multi-million-dollar players.

The winter Games

A_LL SPORTS AT THE winter Olympic Games take place on ice or snow. Competitors at Salt Lake City in 2002 took part in eight sports and groups of sports. Within these sports there were 78 individual and team events in which medals were won. As in the summer Games, there are some team events in which the competitors compete individually and combine their scores. In other team events, such as curling, they compete together as a team. Curling is similar to bowls. It is played on an ice rink by two teams of four players who slide large stones across the ice towards a target.

Hungarian stamp commemorating Lake Placid 1980

NORDIC SKIING
Cross-country skiing and ski-jumping (shown here by Didier Mollard of France), make up the sport of Nordic skiing. The skiing events, over distances from 5 to 50 km, are divided into classical events and freestyle events, in which a skating action is not allowed.

Brakeman applies the brakes at the end of the run

The sled travels on runners

BOBSLED
The two-man and four-man bobsled events take place on a steep, narrow, ice-covered run consisting of straights and bends. The riders push-start the sled at the top of the run, then jump in as it starts to gather speed. The driver, sitting at the front, steers the sled down the run. The team with the lowest total time over four runs wins. The Swiss two-man team of Gustav Weder and Donat Acklin are shown here winning gold in Lillehammer in 1994.

Rider lies flat on the luge to reduce air resistance

ICE HOCKEY
Fast and action-packed, ice hockey is the only field-type team sport in the winter Olympics programme. There are tournaments for both men and women. Six players, including a goalkeeper, from a team of 20 are allowed on the ice at any one time. This action is from a match between Finland and Russia in 1994.

LUGE
Tyler Seitz of Canada is seen here in the men's single luge event in 1998. A luge is a lightweight sled resembling a toboggan. Lugers ride down the same ice-covered run as the bobsledders. They travel feet first, steering around the bends with small foot and body movements. Luge events are men's and women's singles, and doubles. The riders with the lowest total time over a series of runs win.

SKIING

The traditional men's and women's Alpine events are the downhill (shown here by Peter Runggaldier of Italy), slalom, giant slalom, and super-giant slalom, or "super-G". The combined event consists of a slalom run and a downhill run. Two snowboarding events – super-giant slalom and half-pipe – debuted in 1998. There are two freestyle skiing events – mogul skiing and aerials, in which skiers do tricks, spins, and somersaults as they jump off a snow ramp.

Downhill skiers reach speeds in excess of 140 km/h (87 mph)

The bottom of skis is waxed to reduce friction and make the skis slide over the snow and ice more easily

Ski poles are made of lightweight metal tubes

Biathletes shoot both standing up and lying down, or prone

The sled has a lightweight streamlined body for speed

FIGURE SKATING

Figure skating takes place on an oval ice rink. Skaters move around the ice to music, performing glides, steps, spins, and jumps, and are awarded marks by judges. There are men's, women's, and pairs events, made up of a short, or original, programme and a long, or free, programme. Ice dancing is skated in pairs. The emphasis is on musical interpretation, and no high jumps or lifts are allowed. Ice dancing has two compulsory dances and a free programme.

American skater Nancy Kerrigan performing in the 1994 Olympics

Speed skaters wear a helmet in case they fall

Short-track speed skaters can touch the ice for balance around corners

BIATHLON

In the biathlon, competitors ski around a cross-country course, stopping every few kilometres to shoot at targets. For example, in the women's 15 km race, shown here, competitors stop four times, taking five shots each time. The fastest time wins, and a missed target is penalized by a time penalty or a lap of a short penalty loop.

SPEED SKATING

Long-track speed skating is held on a 400-m (437-yd) oval track. Competitors skate in pairs against the clock over distances between 500 and 10,000 m. In short-track speed skating (shown here by the Korean Jun-Ho Lee) competitors race against each other around a tight, 111-m (122-yd) track. Race distances are 500 and 1000 m for individuals and 3000 m for the relays.

The Paralympics

THE SUMMER AND WINTER Paralympic Games are the foremost sports meetings for athletes with physical and mental disabilities. They are held in the same year and in the same host city as the summer and winter Olympics. The "Para" in Paralympics signifies that these Games run beside the Olympics, complementing them. Athletes compete in one of several categories, depending on their particular disability. Currently, there are 18 sports in the summer Games and four in the winter Games.

SILVER MEDAL
This medal from the 1992 Barcelona Paralympics has Braille lettering for the blind, and ordinary lettering.

A helmet similar to a cycling helmet is worn in case of a crash at high speed

Athlete needs strong arms and upper body

Women marathon athletes reach speeds of more than 60 km/h (35 mph)

Legs tucked underneath the body

British marathon racer Rose Hill

Wheel with which the athlete pushes the chair forwards

WHEELCHAIR RACES
Paralympians race in wheelchairs over all the standard distances from the 100 m to the marathon. Racing wheelchairs are as specialized as racing bicycles. Athletes steer by the front wheel, and for track races the steering can be adjusted so that a simple flick of a lever steers the chair around bends.

FENCING
Paralympic fencers, shown here competing in Barcelona in 1992, compete in three disciplines: foil, épée, and sabre. Fencers sit in wheelchairs that are bolted to the floor to prevent them from tipping over. They attack by leaning forwards and defend by leaning back.

LONG JUMP
There are jumping events in several disability categories. Shown here is Ricardo Ignacia of Brazil, competing in the long jump for amputees. He is wearing a specialized artificial limb, or prosthesis that can stand the pounding of the run-up, take-off, and landing.

BASKETBALL
Wheelchair basketball is one of the original Paralympic events. The majority of rules, such as team size, court size, and basket height, are those set down by the International Basketball Federation. The wheelchairs are designed to allow the players to accelerate and spin quickly. Intellectual-disability basketball was played for the first time at the Paralympics at Sydney in 2000.

Bar attached to the front wheel for steering

Chair frame is 1.4 m (4.5 ft) long

SPRINTING
This is British athlete Stuart Bryce competing in the 1992 Paralympics. His right leg is amputated above the knee. His prosthesis, complete with standard running shoe, allows him to complete sprint races only about 10 percent more slowly than Olympic champions.

Wheelchair racers wear three layers of gloves to prevent blisters

CYCLING
Road cycling became a Paralympic sport in 1988 and was followed by track cycling in 1996. Athletes compete in three categories – visually impaired, cerebral palsy, and amputees. Blind cyclists compete in road and track races on tandem cycles with a sighted partner. Here, Americans Cara Dunney and Scott Evans compete in the 1996 tandem pursuit.

Comings and goings

Both the summer and winter Games have a set programme. The number of sports and events has gradually increased since the first modern Games in 1896. It took a long time for the programme to become settled. Many sports, including peculiar events such as underwater swimming and rope climbing, were dropped along the way, often after just a brief appearance. Some sports, such as archery and tennis, have been introduced, dropped, and reintroduced years later. Most sports now have men's and women's events, but up until the Second World War only a few women's events were included, and there were none at all in 1896.

TENNIS
The first modern Games featured tennis, which stayed an Olympic sport until 1924. It was then dropped because the IOC and the International Tennis Federation disagreed over the definition of amateurism. It was reintroduced in 1988, and Steffi Graf and Miloslav Mecir won the singles competitions.

A long jumper with weights, from an ancient Greek vase

JUMPING WITH WEIGHTS
The only jumping event at Olympia was the long jump with weights, which was part of the pentathlon. The athlete probably took a short run before swinging the weights forwards to gain momentum for his jump. It may have been a single, double, or triple jump.

THE PANKRATION
Just about any tactics were allowed in the combat event called the pankration, a mixture of wrestling and boxing with no rounds or time limit. Only eye gouging and biting were against the rules, but pankratiasts often got away with both. The idea was to make the opponent submit.

Ancient Games

For at least 50 years, until 728 BC, a short sprint the length of the stadium at Olympia was the only event at the ancient Games. Over the next 500 years, events were gradually added, including more foot races, wrestling, the pentathlon, boxing, horse racing, and chariot racing.

Jumping weight, from the 5th century BC

CHARIOT RACING
Spectacular, hazardous, and popular, chariot-racing took place in the long oval hippodrome. There were events for two- and four-horse teams, colts, and older horses. Chariot owners employed drivers to take part, but if their chariot won, they received the glory themselves. The only way women could win medals was by being successful chariot owners.

Charioteer stood on a footplate

Chariot races ranged from about 4 km to more than 12 km (2.5 to 8 miles)

Horse on the other side of the pole is missing

Most chariots were made of wood, wickerwork, and leather

Roman bronze model of a two-horse chariot

Early modern Games

When the modern Olympics were in their infancy, there were many changes to the sports programme from one Games to the next. The hosts added sports that were popular in their country and dropped ones that were unpopular.

Pigeon shooting was dropped as an Olympic sport because too many birds were killed

PIGEON SHOOTING

Olympic shooting events were originally closely linked to the kills needed for warfare and hunting. In Paris in 1900, shooting at live pigeons made its only appearance. Trap-shooting, in which competitors shoot at clay discs called clay pigeons, thrown into the air, is a current event.

TUG-OF-WAR

In tug-of-war, shown here making its last Olympic appearance in 1920, two teams pull on opposite ends of a thick rope, each trying to pull the other over a central line. In 1900, Denmark and Sweden joined forces to win gold when neither was able to form a team on its own.

RUGBY

Rugby football was played when the Olympics were hosted by rugby-playing nations. It did not appear in Athens in 1896, St Louis in 1904, or Stockholm in 1912, and it was dropped after 1924. Other team sports that made a brief appearance in the early modern Olympics include polo and cricket.

Early rugby balls were rounder than modern balls

Recent Games

The Olympic programme continues to expand. Events added recently include traditional sports, such as tennis, and newly established sports, such as snowboarding. International governing bodies make representations to the IOC for their sport to be included. To be part of the summer Games, a sport must be played in 75 countries from four continents for men, and in 40 countries from three continents for women.

Curling stones weigh up to 20 kg (44 lb)

CURLING

The centuries-old game of curling was introduced to the winter Olympics at Nagano in 1998. In curling, players slide a polished stone along the ice, trying to make it stop in the centre of a target. The sport probably originated in Scotland but is most popular in Canada.

TAEKWONDO

Loosely translated, taekwondo means "the art of kicking and punching". Bouts are fought in rounds, and points are scored by striking the opponent's trunk and face. The sport originated in Korea and made its debut as an Olympic medal sport in 2000.

SYNCHRONIZED SWIMMING

As shown here by the Italian team in 1996, synchronized swimmers move in the water in time to music and in time with each other. "Synchro" was demonstrated in 1952, but it became a medal sport only in 1984.

Great Olympians

THE HISTORY OF THE Olympics is full of inspirational and heroic performances, but what makes an athlete a great Olympian rather than just a great athlete? It might be winning at two or more Olympics in succession, or winning several events at the same Games. Or perhaps it is simply taking part again and again, or upholding the Olympic ideal of sportsmanship despite losing. Of course, there are many great sportsmen and women who have never won Olympic gold, perhaps because of injury or lack of form at the critical time, or because they were professional in the amateur era, or because their sports were not included in the Olympic programme.

WINNER'S TABLET
This stone records the feats of a Roman athlete, Lucius, who competed "in all the athletic festivals in a manner worthy of victory".

JIM THORPE
Gold medals in both the decathlon and the track-and-field pentathlon (no longer an Olympic event) at Stockholm in 1912, established American Jim Thorpe as the greatest all-round athlete of the time. He went on to play major-league baseball and American football.

Summer Olympians

Every summer Olympics is remembered for one or more great performances on a track, in the pool, or in the gymnastics hall. Most prominence is given to athletes who win classic events, such as the 100 m or the marathon. Winners in the less well-known sports, such as shooting and yachting, are often the unsung heroes of the Games.

JESSE OWENS
The name of Jesse Owens, seen here in a still from Leni Riefenstahl's film *Olympia*, will always be associated with the Berlin Olympics of 1936. Under the gaze of the racists of the Nazi regime, Owens won gold in the 100 m, 200 m, long jump, and 4 x 100 m relay, setting two Olympic records and a world record.

EMIL ZATOPEK
At the 1952 Games in Helsinki, Czechoslovakian army officer and distance runner Emil Zátopek, seen here leading a heat of the 5000 m, became the only athlete in Olympic history to win gold in the 5000 m, 10,000 m, and marathon at the same Games.

Simple heel outline

Thin leather sole with spikes

Soft leather upper

Emil Zátopek's running shoe

PAAVO NURMI
Finnish middle-distance runner Paavo Nurmi, seen here on the shoulder of his great rival Ville Ritola, was one of the first runners to take a scientific approach to his training. It helped him to win a total of 12 Olympic medals, nine of them gold, at the 1920, 1924, and 1928 Olympics. In 1924, he won the 1500 m and recovered in time to win the 5000 m less than an hour later.

Synthetic upper and laces

Athletics shoes of the 1980s were more supportive and shock-absorbent than those worn by Zátopek in the 1950s

Padded heel

Carl Lewis's running shoe

Carl Lewis's signature

Carl Lewis competing in Seoul in 1988

nni Grey competed several different stances

CARL LEWIS
American sprinter and long jumper Carl Lewis was at the top of his form throughout the 1980s. His greatest Olympic year was 1984, when he won the 100 m, the 200 m, the long jump, and the sprint relay, matching the feat of Jesse Owens in 1936. He retained his 100 m and long jump titles in 1988 and won another relay gold in 1992.

ANNI GREY
ritish wheelchair
hlete Tanni Grey, seen here winning gold the 400 m at Barcelona in 1992, is one of e great Paralympians. She won her first edal, a bronze, in Seoul in 1988, added ur golds in Barcelona, and just missed t on a medal in Atlanta in 1996.

NADIA COMANECI
Having started gymnastic training aged just 6, Romanian gymnast Nadia Comaneci developed a perfect sense of timing and balance. At age 14 she won three Olympic golds, including the all-round title, at Montreal in 1976. She was the first gymnast ever to be awarded a perfect mark of 10.00 at the Olympics, which she achieved on the parallel bars.

Lewis ran the 100 m in Seoul in 9.92 seconds, winning gold after Ben Johnson was disqualified

33

Continued on next page

REDGRAVE AND PINSENT
In Atlanta in 1996, rower Steve Redgrave (left) won gold for the fourth Olympics in a row. It was his second win in the coxless pairs event with Matthew Pinsent. In 1988 he won the same event with Andrew Holmes, and in 1984 he won the coxed fours event. In Sydney he won gold number five in the coxless pairs.

Goggles were worn in the 1960s but no helmet

Ski poles are used for balanc in turns

Two-piece outf instead of th one-piece outf worn b today skie

MARK SPITZ
Munich 1972 saw one of the greatest Olympic performances of all. American swimmer Mark Spitz won all four individual events he entered – the 100 and 200 m freestyle and the 100 and 200 m butterfly – all in world-record times. In winning three relay golds as well, he became the first athlete to win seven golds in one Olympics. He also won two relay golds in Mexico City in 1968.

Weissmuller was the first man to swim 100 m (109 yd) in less than 1 minute

JOHNNY WEISSMULLER
American swimmer Johnny Weissmuller was most famous for his role of Tarzan in the series of films of the 1930s and 1940s. Before movie stardom he won five Olympic golds – three in 1924 (the 100 and 400 m freestyle and the 800 m relay) and two in 1928 (the 100 m freestyle and the 800 m relay). He also won a bronze medal in 1924 as part of the US water-polo team.

Johnny Weissmuller as Tarzan

FANNY BLANKERS-KOEN
Dutch sprinter Fanny Blankers-Koen was the most successful woman athle at the London Olympics of 1948. She won gold in the 80 m hurdles, the 100 and 200 m, and the 4 x100 m relay. At the time, she held seven world record including the long jump and high jump, neither of which she entere at the Games. Mother of tw she was nicknamed "the flying housewife".

Winter Olympians

Heroes and heroines at the winter Olympics include the ice-cool downhill skiers, the graceful and skilful ice skaters, the brave ski-jumpers, and the determined cross-country skiers. A special place in Olympic history is reserved for American speed skater Eric Heiden, who, in 1980, won gold in all five individual events, a feat never accomplished before.

Metal fasteners

Thick soles lock into bindings on the skis

Killy's ski boots of 1968

JEAN-CLAUDE KILLY
French skier Jean-Claude Killy was brought up in the French ski resort of Val-d'Isère. At the age of 24 he won all three Alpine skiing golds (the downhill, slalom, and giant slalom) at the Grenoble Olympics in 1968. He became a member of the IOC in 1995.

Jean-Claude Killy carving a tight turn in the 1967 World Cup

Sonja Henie posing for the cameras

Katarina Witt's skimpy costumes in 1988 brought some criticism from the judges

KATARINA WITT
At the Calgary winter Olympics of 1988, Katarina Witt, then competing for East Germany, took gold in the women's figure skating to retain the Olympic title she had won in Sarajevo four years earlier. She became the first skater since Sonja Henie to retain the title and was given a special award by the IOC.

Katarina Witt performing in the 1988 Olympics

SONJA HENIE
Norwegian figure skater Sonja Henie was a child prodigy in figure skating. She won the Norwegian title aged just 10 and entered the 1924 Olympics aged 12. She won three successive Olympic golds in 1928, 1932, and 1936. She also won every world championship from 1927 to 1936, and went on to star in 11 Hollywood movies.

RAISA SMETANINA
Cross-country skier Raisa Smetanina is the top medal winner in the winter Olympics. She won four gold medals, five silvers, and one bronze over four Olympiads between 1976 and 1988. She competed first for the USSR and then for the Unified Team in 1992.

Getting fit

Performing at the Olympic Games is the dream of all athletes. When the chance comes, they must be at the top of their form so that they can give of their best. For years, diet was not considered an important part of training programmes. Now it is known that it is as important as the shoes the athletes wear. Athletes must keep well hydrated and maintain stores of energy in their muscles. They must eat a balanced diet containing all the vitamins and minerals essential for good health. Shown here is a typical day's food that a decathlete in training needs to eat.

Large glass of water

8.00 AM – BREAKFAST
On waking, athletes should drink a large glass of water to re-hydrate the body after the night. They would then have a small breakfast to stop them from feeling hungry during an early training session and to top up energy levels, especially the blood sugar. Vitamin C in the orange juice helps the body to absorb the iron in the cereal. Too little iron in the blood can lead to anaemia.

Orange juice

143 ml (0.25 pt) semi-skimmed milk

40 g (1.4 oz) high-energy balanced cereal

Stretching exercises warm up the muscles before training

9.00 - 11.30 AM – TRAINING
During a heavy training session, athletes must replace fluid lost through sweating because if they get dehydrated they will tire quickly and may risk injury. A large loss of fluid can affect their health. Isotonic sports drinks contain water, carbohydrates, and sodium and are effective at re-hydrating the body, especially if fluid losses are great.

Banned substances

Some athletes are so keen to win that they take drugs or special potions that make them stronger and faster. Not only is this cheating, but it can also be dangerous to the athletes' health. The use of "aids" such as performance-enhancing drugs and human growth hormones is therefore banned by international and national sports bodies.

1 l (1.75 pt) still sports drink

0.5 l (0.88 pt) still sports drink

11.30 AM – MID-MORNING SNACK
Athletes have a big appetite because they need a lot of energy. They could not survive on only three meals a day, so they have snacks too. As soon as possible after a training session they eat food that is high in carbohydrates, such as bread and bananas, to refuel their muscles – lots of athletes eat while they are changing.

2 teaspoons of honey

Large banana, 120 g (4.2 oz) without skin

Low-fat spread

4 slices thick-sliced white bread, toasted

DRUG TESTING
Every medal winner at the Olympics has to give a urine sample, which is tested for banned substances in a laboratory. Athletes who use banned substances find better and better ways of hiding the fact, so drug-testing procedures have to improve too.

2 large glasses of water

2.00 PM – AFTERNOON MEAL
Athletes in training should have a meal early in the afternoon to allow time for the food to be digested before a run. The meal should contain carbohydrates, protein, and a little fat. Protein and fats build and repair the body. An orange every day supplies a good intake of natural vitamin C. A diet should also include calcium for strong bones and teeth – milk, cheese, and yoghurt are good sources. Some athletes feel that their diet does not contain enough vitamins and minerals, so they take supplements.

60 g (2 oz) Cheddar cheese

Large orange, 210 g (7.4 oz)

2 medium-size baked potatoes, 320 g (11.3 oz)

_330 ml (0.6 pt)_
sports drink

**4.00. PM –
AFTERNOON SNACK**
About an hour and a
half before going for
an evening run, an athlete
would top up on fluid and
carbohydrates. This chocolate
bar is a good source of
carbohydrates.

_Chocolate
bar_

The 1996 3000 m
steeplechase
silver medalist,
Moses Kiptanui,
running near his
home in Kenya

_large
banana,
120 g (4.2 oz)
without skin_

5.30 - 6.30 PM – RUN
For an hour's run at low
intensity, athletes would not carry
a drink. In warm weather, they
would probably take a water bottle
or leave a drink somewhere en route.

_large glass
of water_

7.15 PM – EVENING MEAL
Soon after a run, an athlete has an
evening meal. The food shown
here is for a meal of chicken
stir-fry with pasta, and
yoghurt. As usual, it
contains lots of
carbohydrates,
moderate amounts of
protein, and some fat.
The fruit and vegetables
contain anti-oxidants,
which can ward off
illnesses like colds.
These would affect an
athlete's vital training
schedule.

Training

Athletes may compete for only a few
minutes or even seconds. With the help of
a coach, they train to be in peak condition
at exactly the right time. Their aim is to
perform to their best ability on the day,
and if they are lucky to win a medal.

WIND RESISTANCE
Technique is as important as fitness in competition.
Athletes practise again and again, trying to reach
perfection. In 1997, the British skier Graham
Bell tested his downhill position for wind
resistance in a wind tunnel made to test
the wind resistance of Formula 1 cars.

_150 g (5.3 oz)
low-fat fruit
yoghurt_

_150 g (5.3 oz)
breast of
chicken
without skin_

_Unlimited
assorted
vegetables_

_Large portion
of pasta, 350 g
(12.4 oz) cooked_

WEIGHT TRAINING
Injury can mean months out of action
and many more months of training to
reach top condition again. The US skier
Picabo Street had her knee rebuilt after
an accident but was determined to
compete in the 1998 Games. After hard
work, she won gold in the giant slalom.

_200 g (7 oz)
chopped
canned
tomatoes_

_160 g (5.6 oz)
sweet-and-
sour sauce_

9.00 PM – EVENING SNACK
To make sure they do not go to bed hungry, athletes may
have a sandwich and a hot drink about two hours after the
evening meal. White bread is best because it is not so high
in fibre as brown bread, and is therefore less bulky. Athletes
have to be careful about how much fat they have during
the day, because the body cannot easily turn fat into energy.
They would therefore use a low-fat spread on the bread in
their evening and mid-morning snack, rather than butter.

_Peanut
butter_

_Mug of tea
made with
semi-skimmed
milk_

_2 slices of thick-
sliced white bread_

Low-fat spread

Shapes and sizes

JUST LIKE ALL human beings, sportsmen and women come in different shapes and sizes. For some sports, they develop a certain shape from training and competing, because the more a muscle is used, the more powerful and larger it becomes. For other sports, some natural shapes are more suitable than others. For example, a woman who stands 1.5 m (4 ft 10 in) tall and weighs 38 kg (6 st) would not be good at shot putting, which needs strength and physical power. She would be better at gymnastics, which needs balance and agility.

Weight-lifters develop powerful legs and shoulders. Their arms must not be too long or too short, because this makes it more difficult for them to lift the bar above their head. They have a compact body to maximize their strength and balance.

Arm muscles are used in the final stage of a lift

Side view of weight-lifter

Wrist and fingers do a lot of work, so they are strong and supple

Gymnasts must have complete muscle control

Gymnasts work in bare feet

Strong legs are important for all the disciplines

Knee and ankle joints have to withstand sudden pressure as the lifter stands with the weight

The thick muscle in the buttocks, called the gluteus maximus, moves the legs

Feet have to support massive weights

GYMNAST
Most gymnasts are fairly short and light to enable them to balance, bend, swing, and jump in the different disciplines. Gymnasts use the whole body to make shapes, so they must be strong and supple all over.

The impact of running and jumping is absorbed by cushioning in the shoes

38

Swimmers wear caps to cut down resistance

Deltoid muscle lifts the arm

SPEED SKATER
Speed skaters use the leg muscles more than any others, so their legs and buttocks become well developed. Long arms help them to balance as they skate around the bends, and powerful shoulders help to pump the arms when extra speed is needed.

Pectoral muscle helps move the shoulder

Biceps and triceps bend and straighten the elbow

Strong lungs help swimmers to hold their breath underwater for as long as possible

ALL-ROUND ATHLETE
A decathlete has to be good at 10 different events. He needs to develop strength, speed, agility, and endurance and not concentrate on the attributes needed for one discipline. For example, he must not increase his body weight just to help him in the shot put, because too much weight would slow him down in the speed events.

Strong stomach muscles help the rest of the body to work

Strong upper leg for kicking through the water

SWIMMER
It takes strength to push through water because water resistance is much greater than air resistance. Competition swimmers therefore have strong muscles in the upper back that lift the arms and move the shoulders. Muscles in the upper legs bend and straighten the knees and hips.

Strong, flexible shoulders are needed for throwing the javelin

Muscles in the waist, abdomen, and lower back link the movements of the upper and lower body and are used in all athletics

Hamstring muscles in the back of the leg straighten the hip and bend the knee. A pulled or torn hamstring is one of the most common injuries in athletics

The muscle in the calf bends the foot down when the athlete runs

39

Changing styles

OVER THE PAST 100 YEARS, athletes' fashions have changed, not only in the cut of their clothing but in the fabrics too. Heavy wool shirts and flannel shorts have become light, stretchy one-piece outfits. Shoes are made no longer of stiff leather but of flexible synthetic materials. Athletes today probably train in clothes that weigh less than a running outfit of 1900. It is now recognized that the wrong clothing can slow down a runner, and a tenth of a second can make the difference between gold and nothing.

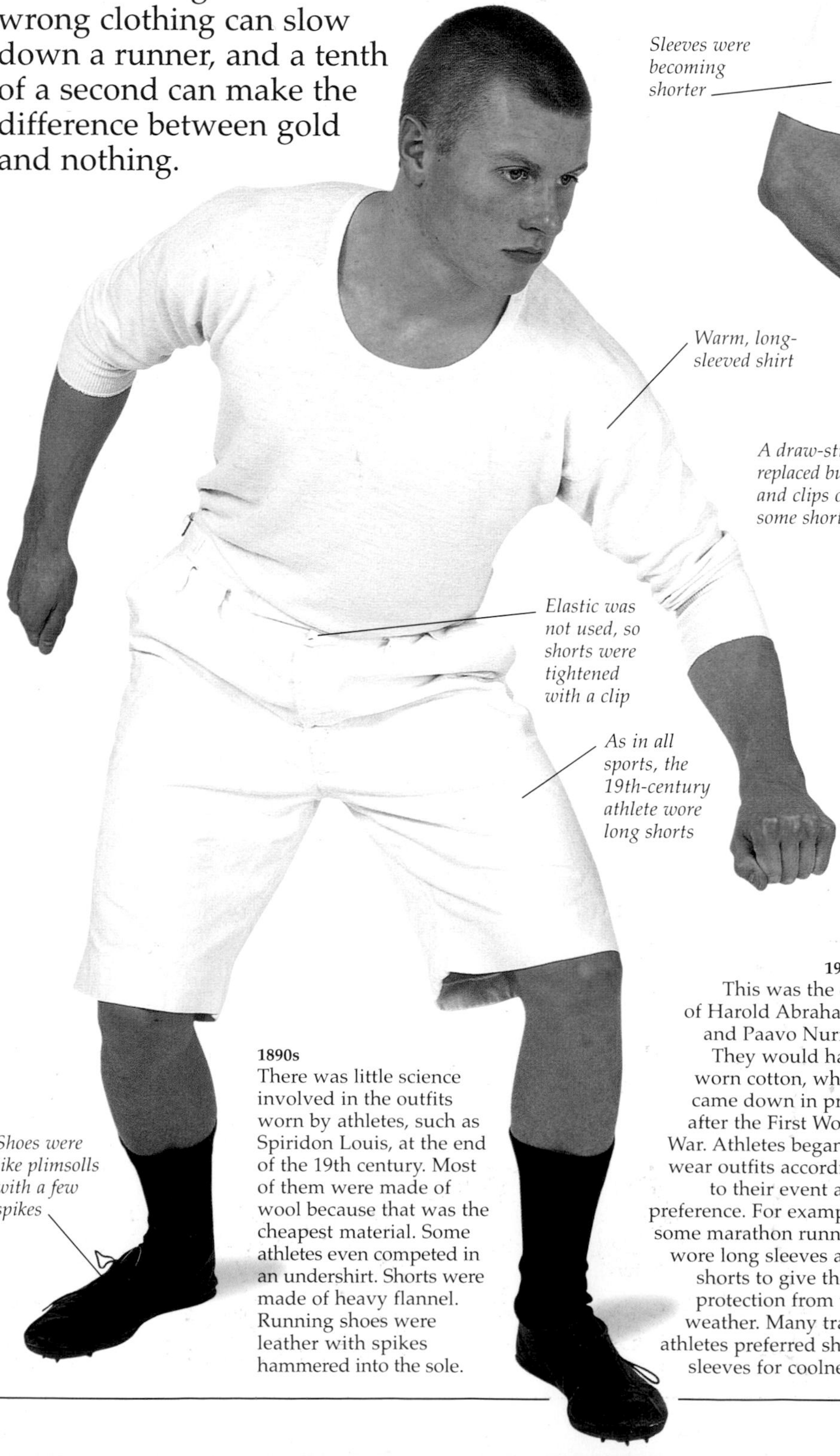

Buttons at the front

Sleeves were becoming shorter

Warm, long-sleeved shirt

A draw-string replaced buttons and clips on some shorts

Elastic was not used, so shorts were tightened with a clip

As in all sports, the 19th-century athlete wore long shorts

Shorts became less baggy

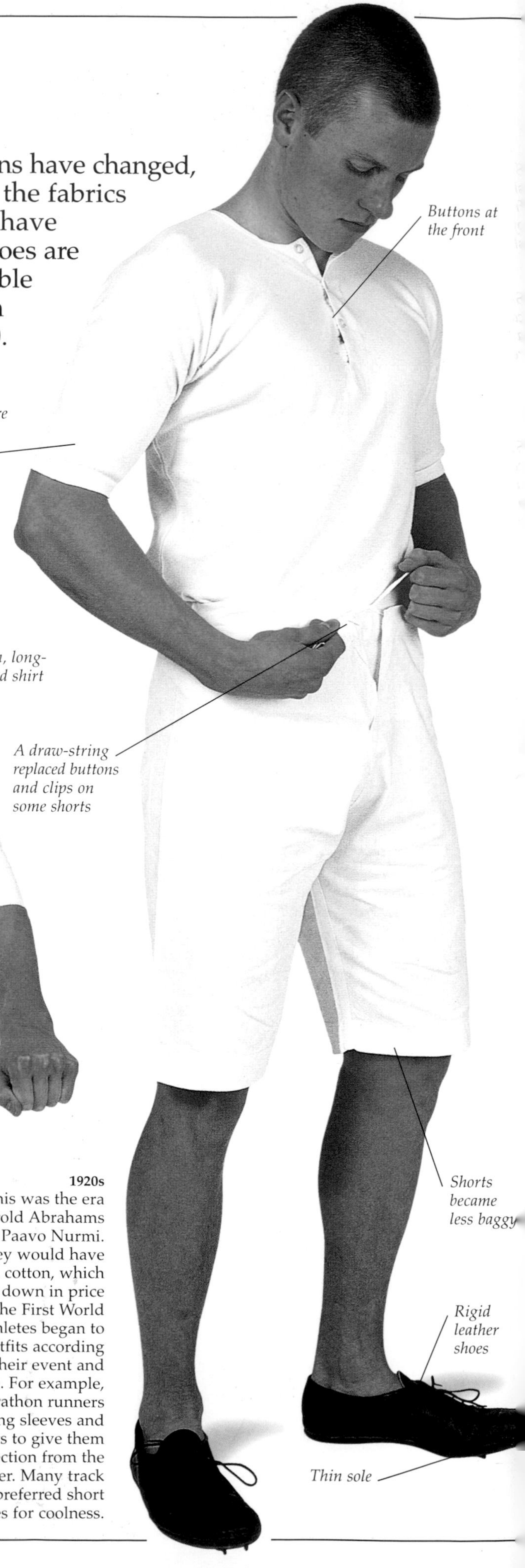

1920s
This was the era of Harold Abrahams and Paavo Nurmi. They would have worn cotton, which came down in price after the First World War. Athletes began to wear outfits according to their event and preference. For example, some marathon runners wore long sleeves and shorts to give them protection from the weather. Many track athletes preferred short sleeves for coolness.

1890s
There was little science involved in the outfits worn by athletes, such as Spiridon Louis, at the end of the 19th century. Most of them were made of wool because that was the cheapest material. Some athletes even competed in an undershirt. Shorts were made of heavy flannel. Running shoes were leather with spikes hammered into the sole.

Shoes were like plimsolls with a few spikes

Rigid leather shoes

Thin sole

1950s

Sleeveless shirts became common in the 1950s, when Emil Zátopek was at his peak. They were cool and comfortable. Nylon shorts were popular because they were light. Different-coloured shorts and shirts were worn by different athletes as part of a national "uniform".

2000s

The Olympic Games today are full of colour. The uniforms of each nation are specially designed, often incorporating the colours and designs on the national flag. With the help of scientific research, clothes and shoes are made to help athletes perform their best.

Sleeveless shirts allowed free movement of the arms and shoulders

Shirt caused only a little wind resistance

Stripes of varying colours and widths identified an athlete's country

Spikes for giving grip on the track

Short shorts were easier to run in

The wearing of socks was a matter of preference

Modern material helps moisture to evaporate

Stretch outfit hugs the body, cutting down wind resistance

Thigh-length suit keeps the upper legs warm, reducing muscle strain

Considerable scientific research now goes into the production of sports shoes

SPECIALIZED SPRINT SHOES

Modern sprint shoes are made of lightweight synthetic material for maximum flexibility and comfort. They are designed to support the feet in the right places and absorb the impact from the ground.

Sloping toe helps the sprinter to run correctly

Made to measure

S AFETY IN SPORT is important, but so too are speed and comfort. Designers today spend many hours of expensive research creating sports clothes that look good, give protection and comfort, and help athletes achieve great performances. They take advantage of research in other fields and have even used materials developed for use in Space. Every sport has its own requirements. Some outfits must absorb impacts, some must be aerodynamic, others must be smart. Improvements happen quickly, and today's athletes would be horrified by the clothes of just 10 years ago.

BASEBALL
Baseball catchers and the home plate umpire wear chest and head protection against deflections off the bat. These may come at 140 km/h (87 mph).

SWIMMING GOGGLES
Modern swimming goggles are shaped to fit tightly around the eyes so that they do not let in water or mist up. Swimmers wear goggles to protect their eyes from chlorine in the water and to allow them to see where they are going.

SWIMWEAR
This 1920s swimming costume may look similar to the blue one of the 1990s, but the two are in fact quite different. In the 1920s, costumes were made of cotton. They would have become heavy when wet and, because they did not fit tightly, would have slowed the swimmers down. Today, costumes are made to cling to the body and allow water to flow past quickly, helping swimmers to cut vital fractions of seconds off their race times.

Mask protects the face from fast-travelling pucks

One glove has webbing between the fingers, while the stick hand has extra protection

These old-fashioned gloves do not have the same style of thumbs as modern gloves, which have been designed to prevent eye gouging

Legs could be tightened with a draw-string

1920s swimming costume

Material stays close to the body even when wet

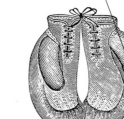

BOXING GLOVES
Boxers wear gloves to protect the opponent. Big, heavy gloves absorb much of the power of punches before they hit the opponent, and spread the impact of the blows. Before a fight, both boxers' gloves are weighed to make sure they are the same.

ICE HOCKEY PADDING
Ice hockey is the world's fastest team sport. The goalkeepers wear huge pads on their legs and arms to protect them from the puck, which can be hit at more than 200 km/h (124 mph). They also wear masks that protect the head, neck, and throat.

Modern costume is made of special low-resistant material with stripes that water runs down easily

Long legs, as in the costume of the 1920s

1990s swimming costume

DRESSAGE OUTFIT

Riders in dressage events wear formal clothes and have to be as well turned out as their horse. The standard outfit is a jacket with tails, a coloured waistcoat, and cream or white breeches with matching gloves. Riders wear a top hat rather than a helmet, which they wear in other equestrian events for safety.

Top hat looks smarter than a crash helmet

White stock fastened with a stock pin

Jean-Claude Killy's skiing helmet

Bronze wrestler from the 3rd century BC

Stretch breeches allow close contact with the horse

Long leather boots

SKIING HELMET

Skiers can have crashing falls, and good head protection is vital. Killy's helmet in the 1960s was not as efficient as today's lighter helmets, which give more protection to the head and neck. They are also more aerodynamic, allowing the skiers to go even faster.

This mask would have allowed the tip of a weapon to go through the mesh

ANCIENT WRESTLER'S CAP

In ancient times, wrestlers wore caps to prevent their opponents from grabbing their hair. Today, hair pulling is illegal, but grabbing clothes is not. Competitors therefore wear tight-fitting clothes, which are difficult to grab hold of.

FENCING MASK

The founder of the modern Olympic Games, Pierre de Coubertin, enjoyed fencing, but his mask would have been forbidden in today's competitions. Modern helmets have a transparent plastic film over the mesh for extra safety and cover the whole head.

Fencing mask of Pierre de Coubertin

Strap fixes securely over the top of the shoe

Wooden heel

Weight-lifters can choose whether or not to wear a belt

WEIGHT-LIFTING EXTRAS

Some weight-lifters wear a special belt when they are attempting a lift. The belt provides something on which the stomach muscles can press. Shoes have a wooden heel for pushing down on the floor, a rubber sole for grip, and a strong support strap over the top of the foot.

Wheels of fortune

THE EQUIPMENT for wheel sports has probably changed more than any other equipment used in the Olympics. Advances in gears, tyres, brakes, and lightweight materials, particularly over the last 20 years, have improved racing bicycles by leaps and bounds. Bicycles are now made specifically for different events, such as track racing, road racing, pursuit, and mountain biking. Modern racing wheelchairs have also taken advantage of these developments and, like racing bikes, look completely different from their "everyday" counterparts seen on the street.

A modern racing wheelchair weighs only about 8 kg (18 lb)

Steering can be set up to make the chair go around a track perfectly in one lane

Tyres are 19 mm (0.75 in) wide

Athlete punches the outside ring around to move the chair forwards

MODERN RACING WHEELCHAIR
Racing wheelchairs have developed from standard upright chairs, through long, four-wheeled chairs to the modern three-wheeled "chariots". Before a race, each chair is checked by officials to make sure its specifications, such as length and size of wheels, fall within the regulations.

High handlebars would have put the rider in a wind-resistant, upright position

Metal frame

Thick tyres would have gripped well but would have made the bike slow

1890s
Bicycles used in the first Olympic Games must have been uncomfortable to ride. The handlebars were at the same height as the saddle with little space in the middle, so the rider would have been rather cramped with his weight over the back wheel. This bike has only one gear and no brakes – like track racing bicycles today.

Hard leather saddle offered little comfort

Drop handlebars with brake levers

Wheels were fixed with an early, quick-release mechanism

The bike had three gears

1930s
Bicycles gradually became more streamlined. The horizontal crossbar and longer wheelbase of this bike allowed the rider to take up a less wind-resistant position and made pedalling easier and more efficient.

Toe straps kept the rider's feet on the pedals

A one-piece frame is more streamlined than a frame made of several tubes

1990s
The British cyclist Chris Boardman became the 4000 m individual pursuit champion in the 1992 Games in Barcelona. Made of carbon-fibre with titanium and aluminium parts, his bike was extremely light. The revolutionary design, shown in this replica, was controversial, but because the chain was outside the frame it was within the regulations. Pursuit racers have to cycle as fast as possible to try to catch up with an opponent who starts on the opposite side of the track. In the final, Boardman uniquely caught his opponent with a lap to go.

Boardman rested his forearms on the long handlebars

LOTUS *Sport*

The frame was purpose-built to suit the rider

Three-spoked wheel on the front is less likely to behave like a sail than a disc wheel

MAVIC

3G

Bike has one speed only

The steep seat tube positions the rider further over the bottom bracket, increasing pedalling efficiency

Solid disk wheels are stronger and more aerodynamic than spoked wheels

Riders sit in a racing crouch over the low handlebars to reduce drag, or wind resistance

ENER·D.M.

Gear levers

1980s
This aluminium bicycle was used by the winning Italian team in the 1984 100 km team time trial. Team-trial bikes need to be aerodynamic and light. Team members race in a tight group in the slip-stream of the leader, who moves to the back every few seconds, as a different rider takes the lead.

Bottom bracket

Small front wheel reduces drag, weighs less than a large wheel, and needs less frame in which to mount it, making the bike lighter

45

Skates and skis

THE EQUIPMENT USED IN the first winter Olympic Games in 1924 at Chamonix, France, is almost unrecognizable compared with that used at the dawn of the 21st century. Light, strong, synthetic materials, such as fibreglass, have been developed to replace wood and iron. Leather skating boots have become softer and more comfortable without losing their support. Winter sports can be dangerous, and equipment is now designed with safety in mind as much as speed. Skiers, skaters, and bobsled riders go much faster than their early counterparts, but they face far less risk of injury or death.

Shoe is fixed to the blade with leather and metal

FIRST EVENT
The men's speed skating 500 m was the first event to be decided in the first winter Olympic Games in 1924. The blade on this early skate is curved up at the toe. The curve was removed on later speed skates.

RAISED ON HIGH
Speed skating takes place around an oval track. The two skaters have to swap lanes along the back straight of each lap to make sure they both skate the correct distance. The boot of this early speed skate is raised above the blade. This allowed the skater to lean inward around the corners.

Long single-edged blade helped the skater to start quickly and maintain high speed

Boot is fixed to metal struts on the blade

Speed skating

Traditional speed skating is a graceful sport, with the skaters taking smooth, powerful strokes. They race against the clock at speeds of up to 56 km/h (34 mph). Short-track speed skating is more aggressive because the skaters race against each other.

Boot has Velcro fastenings

Early wooden ski

Fibreglass ski, pre 195

SPEED SKATE
Speed skater race in on direction aroun a track. The do not nee to perform any specia movements

SHORT-TRACK SPEED SKATE
This short-track speed skate was used in 1988 when the sport was demonstrated at the winter Olympics. Short-track speed skating was an Olympic competition sport for the first time in 1992 at Albertville, France.

Blade made of steel

Sled is made of wood

To reduce wind resistance, the crew keep their heads below the sides of the sled

EARLY BOBSLED
Bobsleds were invented in the 1880s, when someone lashed two toboggans together. The first Olympic four-man bob competition was held in 1924. A two-man event was first held in 1932.

Bobsledding

There are very few sights in sport as spectacular as a bobsled on the run. Early sleds were open, and the driver steered using a wheel at the front. Riders today are well protected inside the sled.

MODERN BOBSLED
Bobsleds today hurtle down a run at speeds of up to 150 km/h (93 mph). Made of carbon fibre, they are light and aerodynamic. Two man bobs must not exceed 2.7 m (8.8 ft) in length and 390 kg (860 lb) in weight, including the riders. The limits for four-man bobs are 3.8 m (12.5 ft) and 630 kg (1,389 lb).

Figure skating

The blades on figure skates are hollow-ground to give them an inside and outside edge. They are curved slightly to allow the skaters to change their weight from front to back. All the movements that figure skaters perform rely on these four basic edges.

HIGH JUMPER
The high top of this 1950s figure skate gave a skater ankle support but offered little flexibility. It was in the 1952 Olympics that the American Dick Button showed the world his new jump – the triple loop – which is now a popular jump for men and women.

Leather upper

Fibreglass
ski, pre 1980

Fibreglass
ski, 1990s

Fibreglass
ski, 1990s

KIS THROUGH THE AGES
ki bindings attach the skis to a skier's boots.
hey have changed enormously since the first
lympic Alpine skiing event in 1936, as have
ne skis themselves. Early skis were wooden
nd had a leather strap that buckled around
ne boots. Today's fibreglass skis have clip
indings that release the boot in a fall.

IGURE SKATER
lades for figure
kating are designed
 allow the skaters
 skate in circles,
ırn, jump, and
oin. The
katers move
neir weight to
se the edges.

Serrated section is called a toe rake and is used in toe jumps and toe stops

1990s
Modern ice skates are much more comfortable than early ones. This 1990s skate was almost seven times lighter than the 1950s one. Boots can now be different colours to match the skater's costume.

Fancy footwork

A GOOD PAIR OF SHOES is one of the most important items of sports equipment. Shoes do not just protect the feet but can cut down the stresses on ankle and knee joints too. Olympic athletes today know that not only will they reduce injuries by wearing the right shoes, but their performance will be improved too. A great deal of research and development now goes into the production of a new model of sports shoe, and better materials and shapes are being discovered all the time. This makes the shoes expensive, but being an Olympic athlete does not come cheaply.

Sports shoes

Sports shoes are designed especially for different games. Players who have to run fast, make sudden stops, or kick a ball all require different things from their shoes. Conditions also affect shoe design. For example, basketball shoes would be useless on a muddy soccer pitch, and soccer boots would be dangerous on a clay tennis court.

Perforations let air in and heat out, keeping the foot cool

TENNIS SHOE

Tennis players need shoes with good grip because they have to stop and change direction quickly. Cushioning in the soles protects the feet from the constant jarring caused by running on a hard surface.

SOCCER BOOT

Soccer players need to feel the ball through their boots and have support for their ankles. Good soccer boots are therefore made of soft, flexible leather. They allow players to kick the ball with the inside or outside of their feet. Studs can be changed for different pitch conditions.

Soles have grip to prevent the athlete from slipping

TRAINER (ABOVE)

Each running step uses three times as much force as a walking step. Training shoes have compressed-air shock absorbers in the midsole to reduce stress-related injuries to the foot. Outside conditions can damage the midsole, so some trainers have sell-by dates.

JAVELIN SHOE (LEFT)

Javelin throwers wear a different shoe on each foot, depending on from which one they throw. The athletes land heavily on the heel of one foot just before throwing and then have to stop quickly in front of the foul line. The shoes are tough, with good ankle support and padding around the toe.

Basketball shoe

This modern basketball shoe has been broken down into its many components, each one designed carefully to provide comfort and support to different parts of the foot. The three main components are the upper, the midsole, and the outsole.

Flexible frame for the ankle wrap

High, padded h[eel] gives all-round protection to th[e] back of the foot

Ankle wrap provides ankle stability

PLAYING THE GAME

Basketball players are required to sprint, stop sharply, turn, and of course jump. The match shown here is the United States v Lithuania at Atlanta in 1996. The Lithuanians, in white, eventually won the bronze medal, while the Americans went on to win gold, as expected.

HEEL AND ANKLE PROTECTION

Playing basketball puts great strain on the feet and legs, especially the ankle joints. The heel and ankle area of a basketball shoe must therefore provide support and protection. It must fit perfectly around the heel to prevent blisters as well as more serious injuries.

Tongue extends up the shin for extra support

Soft padding for comfort

Loop can be used to pull on the shoe

Elastic straps are stitched to the inside of the shoe

Holes for laces

UPPER
The upper part of the shoe covers the top of the foot and goes around the side of the foot as far as the ankle. It is made of lightweight synthetic material that allows the foot to breathe inside the shoe.

AS A WHOLE
Many years were spent testing and developing this shoe before it was put into production. Each section was developed by scientists with the help of top players. When all the components are put together, they form a lightweight, top-of-the-range basketball shoe that provides support and freedom of movement – and looks good too.

Midsole

Fluid capsule visible through a "window" in the sole

Heel stabilizer containing cushioning fluid

Lightweight sock-liner

Midsole is reinforced to provide stability

Midsole is shaped to fit the contours of the foot

Capsules containing special fluid provide cushioning and stability underneath the heel and ball of the foot

Fluid capsules fit into recesses in the midsole

Rubber outsole

OUTSOLE
Basketball is played indoors on a smooth wooden court. The rubber tread on the bottom of the sole provides the vital grip players need to prevent them from slipping as they stop and turn quickly.

Perfect timing

1936 STARTING PISTOL
The starting pistols of old fired real shots, although there were no bullets. A hammer hit powder inside the gun, which ignited with a bang. A small plume of smoke came from the gun after it had been fired.

IT WILL TAKE LONGER FOR YOU to read this paragraph than it will take the winners of the men's and women's Olympic 100 m finals to run their race. The time for the men's 100 m is now less than 10 seconds. The improvement in athletes' technique and fitness has helped them to achieve record-breaking performances, but technology has helped too, in the development of synthetic tracks, aerodynamic clothes, and modern shoes. Starting and timing methods have had to keep up, and modern electronic systems help both athletes and officials, by ensuring that every race is as fair as possible.

Modern starting pistol does not make a sound itself

ELECTRONIC GUN
A modern system for starting sprint races uses an electronic gun sound generator. When the starter pulls the trigger of the gun, a signal is passed to the sound generator, which produces a sound and transmits it by cable to a loudspeaker built into the back of each starting block. This ensures that all the athletes hear the signal at the same time.

The start

The start of a race must be fair. Runners in the outside lanes used to be at a disadvantage because the sound of the gun reached them after it reached the inside athlete. Improved starting systems have now eliminated this problem.

ANCIENT START
This is the marble starting sill used in the Pythian Games at Delphi in the 5th century BC. Ancient Greek runners used a standing start with their arms stretched forwards. They gripped the grooves in the sill firmly with their toes.

STARTING BLOCKS
Electronic starting blocks were introduced in the 1980s. Pressure exerted by athletes on the blocks is measured and relayed to the starter. The most advanced system monitors each athlete individually, taking into account weight, sex, and experience. It can tell the difference between a non-deliberate movement and a false start.

Olympic tracks were made of cinder until 1968

Athletes used a trowel to dig a hole in the track behind the starting line

PREPARING FOR THE 100 M IN 1928
Starting blocks as we know them were first authorized in 1938, which meant that they could not be used at the Olympic Games until 1948. Before then, athletes in sprint races dug holes in the track to give them something to push against at the start.

100 M RECORDS
Since 1896, the winning time of the men's Olympic 100 m final has improved by more than 2 seconds. The first women's 100 m took place in 1928, and their time has improved by slightly less.

	1896	1900	1908	1924	1928	1936	1948
MEN	T. Burke (USA) 12.0	F. Jarvis (USA) 11.0	R. Walker (S. Afr.) 10.8	H. Abrahams (GB) 10.6	P. Williams (Can.) 10.8	J. Owens (USA) 10.3	H. Dillard (USA) 10.3
WOMEN	-	-	-	-	E. Robinson (USA) 12.2	H. Stephens (USA) 11.5	F. Blankers-K((Neth.) 11.9

CHRONOMETER

In the early part of the 20th century, athletes were timed using a chronometer. This one has three dials fixed to the outside of the box. The dials record hours, minutes, and seconds.

The finish of the 100 m in Tokyo in 1964

Wooden box contains the chronometer's mechanism

100 M FINISH IN 1964

In 1964, an electronic quartz timing system was used at the Olympic Games for the first time. It measured time more accurately than anything that had been used before, and led to the launch of the first quartz watches in 1969. Many timing judges sat at the finish line, each with their own stopwatch.

Quartz sports timer used in 1964

The finish

Athletes and spectators no longer have to wait agonizing seconds to find out who has won which medal. With modern technology, they can learn the placings almost immediately. Athletes can now be timed to within a thousandth of a second.

SLIT-VIDEO FINISH

A new slit-video system now makes it easier than ever before for judges to decide on the winner of the 100 m. The system scans a thin line aligned with the finishing line up to 2,000 times per second, forming a clear image of the athletes crossing the line.

COMPUTER JUDGES

With the slit-video photo-finish system, an image of athletes on the line is immediately displayed on monitors for the judges to study. They move a cursor to the torso of each athlete and read the time from a scale at the bottom of the image. Colour images make it even easier for judges to pick out each athlete.

1952	1960	1968	1976	1984	1992	1996	2000
Remigino (USA) 10.4	A. Hary (W. Ger.) 10.32	J. Hines (USA) 9.95	H. Crawford (Trin.) 10.06	C. Lewis (USA) 9.99	L. Christie (GB) 9.96	D. Bailey (Can.) 9.84	M. Greene (USA) 9.87
M. Jackson (Aus.) 11.5	W. Rudolph (USA) 11.18	W. Tyus (USA) 11.08	A. Richter (W. Ger.) 11.08	E. Ashford (USA) 10.97	G. Devers (USA) 10.82	G. Devers (USA) 10.94	M. Jones (USA) 10.75

Spoilsports

THE OLYMPIC GAMES are major media events and attract international audiences of millions. They therefore present people with an ideal opportunity to bring their protests and grievances to the attention of the whole world. There have been very few summer Olympic Games that have not been affected by international or national politics, and in most cases it is the athletes who have lost out. For almost every summer Games, the politicians of at least one country have withdrawn their team. Other countries have been excluded from some Games by the organizers. The Games of 1916, 1940, and 1944 did not take place at all because of world wars.

Swastika was used as the symbol of the Nazi party

Commemorati med

JAPAN AS HOST
It took almost 20 years for Japan to be fully taken back into the Olympic fold after the Second World War. The choice of Tokyo as host for the 1964 Games showed that the IOC thought Japan had been shunned for long enough, but it was an unpopular choice with many people who remembered the war.

Hitler's soldiers invaded Poland in September 1939, causing Britain and France to declare war on Germany

Antwerp city's badge

Statuette of a German Nazi

THE GREAT WAR
The Games of 1916 were due to be held in Berlin, Germany, but when war broke out in 1914, they had to be cancelled. The first Games to be held after the First World War were in Antwerp, Belgium, in 1920. Germany, Austria, Hungary, and Turkey were not invited because of their part in the war. Antwerp had been occupied by enemy forces only 18 months before the Games began, but the organizing committee still put on a successful Games with a record number of countries and competitors attending.

Many Olympic Games posters depict ancient Greek athletes

VII OLYMPIADE
ANVERS (BELGIQUE)
AOÛT-SEPTEMBRE 1920

Poster advertising the Antwerp Games

SIGN OF SUPPORT
American athletes Tommie Smith and John Carlos came first and third in the 1968 men's 200 m. At the medal ceremony, they showed their support for the Black Power movement's racial equality campaign in America by raising black-gloved clenched fists during the playing of their anthem. They were expelled from the Olympic village.

NAZI PROPAGANDA
The Games of 1936 were held in Berlin, Germany. Adolf Hitler used the Games as a Nazi propaganda exercise. He hoped that blond, blue-eyed, pale-skinned Aryan athletes would win everything, but black Americans won most of the athletics medals. War broke out in 1939, and the Games were not held again until 1948.

MUNICH 1972
On 5 September 1972, Palestinian terrorists burst into the athletes' village in Munich, shot dead two Israeli competitors, and took nine others hostage. The terrorists demanded a helicopter to fly them and the hostages away from the scene, and a rescue mission went horribly wrong. All nine hostages, a German policeman, and five of the Palestinians died in a gun battle at a nearby air-force base.

Helicopter of the German police blown up by the Palestinian terrorists

UGANDA BARRED
Uganda was banned from the 1976 Games in Montreal, Canada, because of its ruler Idi Amin's violations of human rights. He is alleged to have had 100,000 people killed, including swimmers who beat him in races at his palace.

Amin awarded himself lots of medals

General Idi Amin

BOYCOTTS
In December 1979, the Soviet Union invaded Afghanistan. In protest, the USA led a boycott of the Moscow 1980 summer Olympic Games. Many of the Games of the 1970s and 1980s were affected by boycotts. National leaders banned their athletes from competing to protest against the political, military, or sporting actions of countries that were invited.

Amin ruled Uganda from 1971 to 1979

SOUTH AFRICA RETURNS
At Barcelona in 1992, South African athletes competed in the Games for the first time in 25 years. South Africa had been barred because of its apartheid regime, in which black people could not live on equal terms with white people. It was invited back because the political prisoner Nelson Mandela had been freed in 1990, marking the beginning of the end of apartheid.

UNIFIED TEAM
After the breakup of the Soviet Union in the late 1980s, some of the states competed independently in 1992 for the first time in more than 50 years. Athletes from the other Soviet republics, then in the Commonwealth of Independent States, competed as the Unified Team and paraded under the Olympic flag. The team finished second in the winter medals table and top in the summer.

Souvenir pin from Barcelona 1992

Barcelona '92

Behind the scenes

O<small>N</small> 23 S<small>EPTEMBER</small>, 1993, Juan Antonio Samaranch, president of the IOC, announced that Sydney had won the right to host the Games of the XXVII Olympiad. The Olympic Games are the biggest sporting event in the world, and hosting them is an enormous undertaking. As well as the competitions, the organizing committee must arrange transport, accommodation, and security for thousands of people. More than 10,000 competitors and 5,000 support staff from 200 countries attend the Games. Up to 15,000 journalists come to cover the events. The city must also prepare itself for the arrival of tens of thousands of spectators from all over the world. All this costs money, and since 1984, the Olympic movement has allowed host cities to meet the costs with the help of advertising and sponsorship.

A WINNING BID
The Australian delegation cheered when the IOC awarded the 2000 Games to Sydney. Several cities bid for each Games. Members of the IOC consider the bids, then meet to vote seven years before the Games will be held. One bid has to gain more than half of the votes to win.

THE VENUES
Sydney's Olympic plan involved the development of four world-class sporting facilities based on four Olympic precincts including Sydney Olympic Park, shown here under construction. Adequate transport for spectators was vital. Trains and buses carried nearly 80,000 spectators an hour to new terminals only a short walk away from where most of the sports took place.

Weight-lifting

The Olympic rings can be used only on official Olympic items

Sailing

Representation of the Olympic flame

Gymnastics

Field hockey

Archery

Athletics

HOUSING THE ATHLETE
This is the 1998 Olympic "village" for athletes in Nagano. The first village was in Los Angeles in 1932, but it was for men only. In 2000, all the athletes lived together in one village for the first time in Olympic history. After the Olympics it was converted to accommodate 7,000 competitors and officials for the Paralympics. More ramps were built for wheelchair access, and Braille instructions and signs were added.

COMMEMORATIVE COINS
The design and production of commemorative items such as coins, medals, and badges has to be organized well in advance of the Games. These six coins are from a series of coins cut to celebrate the Sydney Games. Each one has been designed to represent a different sport. They may be valuable collectors' items in years to come.

PARIS 1924

VIII° OLYMPIADE

JEUX OLYMPIQUES

Poster for the 1924 Olympic Games in Paris

THE CEREMONIES
After each final, the athletes who were first, second, and third receive their medals in a special ceremony. The organizing committee has to devise the ceremony and make sure that enough medals have been made. The flag and national anthem of all competing nations have to be available.

Dish reflects radio signals from one place to another

The Intelsat 7 satellites provide up to 90,000 voice channels and three TV broadcasts simultaneously

MEDIA COVERAGE
The Olympic Games have a worldwide audience of more than 3.5 billion people. The launching of satellites in Space has meant that the events can be filmed and shown live around the world. Written reports and photographs are now sent through "cyberspace" on the Internet or along telephone lines as faxes.

ADVERTISING THE GAMES
Today, there is probably little need to advertise the Games, but organizing committees still have an advertising budget. At least one poster has been designed for every Games since 1896, and the same design has often been used on the official programmes.

Badge from the 1912 Olympic Games

Badges are sometimes presented to those who have helped at the Games

Olympiska Spelen Stockholm 1912

INTERNATIONAL OLYMPIC COMMITTEE
The IOC consists of people who sit on their own country's Olympic committee. The president of the IOC is one of the most important people in the world of sport. Avery Brundage (left) was president of the IOC in 1972 when terrorists attacked the athletes' village in Munich. After the tragedy he made a speech to say that the Games must go on after a 24-hour break.

THE START OF THINGS TO COME
The Stockholm Olympics of 1912 was one of the two or three best ever and showed the hosts of future Games how it should be done. The organizing committee drew up a full list of events, trained the officials thoroughly, and introduced the use of electric timing devices and public-address systems.

The stadium

THE CENTREPIECE OF ANY OLYMPIC city is the main stadium. For most summer Olympic and Paralympic Games, the stadium hosts the opening and closing ceremonies and the track and field events, including the marathon finish. Sports architects have to consider many different aspects when designing a new stadium. There can be more than 100,000 spectators plus thousands of journalists, athletes, and staff in a stadium at any one time. Safety, crowd flow, comfort, and services in all areas of the stadium have to be considered. The architects use computers to identify any possible problems raised by a design. The computers can even show the view from individual seats before the stadium is built.

Trusses hold up the roof

Four jumbo jets could be parked side by side under the main arch

THE PLAYERS' TUNNEL
Marching into the Olympic Stadium must be a thrilling experience. Ancient Greek athletes would have experienced much the same feeling as they walked up this tunnel to emerge into the stadium at Olympia. The tunnel was 32 m (35 yd) long.

MUNICH STADIUM
Hosting the Games gives cities an excuse to build magnificent new stadiums. Munich's Olympic Stadium was built for the 1972 Games. It can hold 80,000 spectators. Two years after the Games, soccer's World Cup Final was held there.

Moveable seats in the lower seating bowl make it possible for the stadium to host rectangular-arena sports as well as oval-arena sports

In post-Olympic mode, a polycarbonate roof provides cover for 60,000 seats

AFTER THE GAMES
After the Olympics and Paralympics, the Sydney Olympic Stadium was adapted to make it suitable for a variety of sports, such as Australian football, rugby, and soccer. The removal of the north and south upper stands reduced the seating capacity by 30,000.

→N

Plan of the seating for the Sydney Olympics

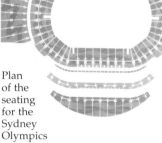

The Olympic soccer final was played on the grass infield

The running track is lower than the front row of seats

18,000 trucks were required to deliver the concrete for the superstructure of the stadium

Athletes enter the arena along a passage between blocks of seats

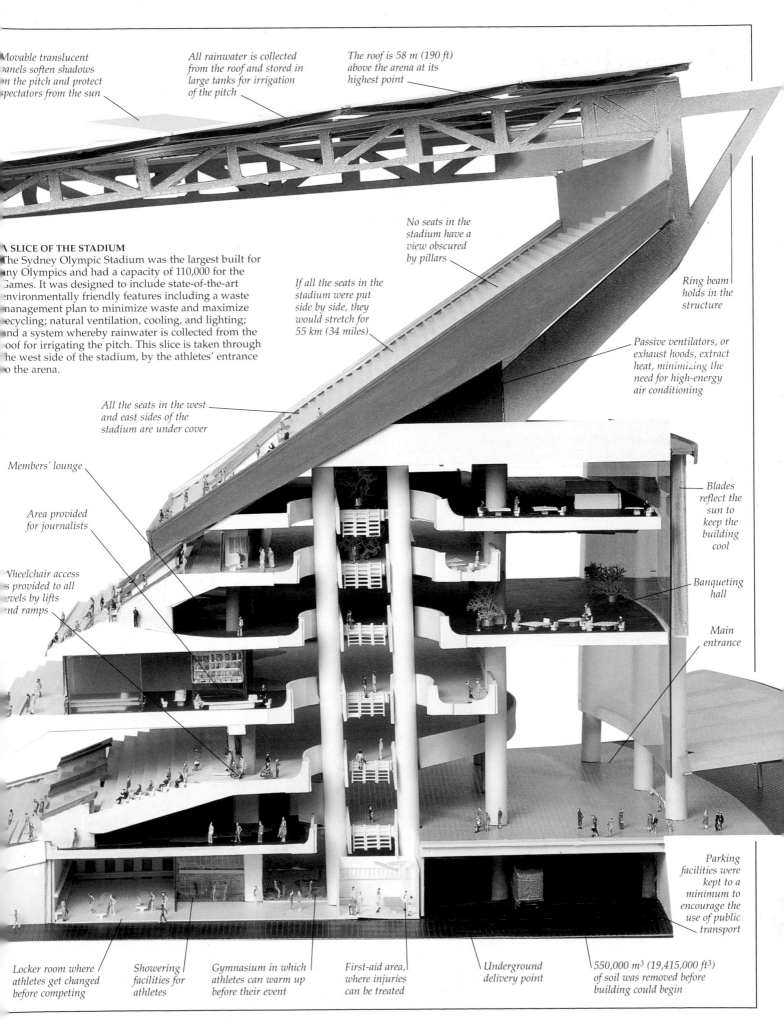

Movable translucent panels soften shadows on the pitch and protect spectators from the sun

All rainwater is collected from the roof and stored in large tanks for irrigation of the pitch

The roof is 58 m (190 ft) above the arena at its highest point

A SLICE OF THE STADIUM

The Sydney Olympic Stadium was the largest built for any Olympics and had a capacity of 110,000 for the Games. It was designed to include state-of-the-art environmentally friendly features including a waste management plan to minimize waste and maximize recycling; natural ventilation, cooling, and lighting; and a system whereby rainwater is collected from the roof for irrigating the pitch. This slice is taken through the west side of the stadium, by the athletes' entrance to the arena.

No seats in the stadium have a view obscured by pillars

Ring beam holds in the structure

If all the seats in the stadium were put side by side, they would stretch for 55 km (34 miles)

Passive ventilators, or exhaust hoods, extract heat, minimizing the need for high-energy air conditioning

All the seats in the west and east sides of the stadium are under cover

Members' lounge

Area provided for journalists

Blades reflect the sun to keep the building cool

Banqueting hall

Main entrance

Wheelchair access is provided to all levels by lifts and ramps

Parking facilities were kept to a minimum to encourage the use of public transport

Locker room where athletes get changed before competing

Showering facilities for athletes

Gymnasium in which athletes can warm up before their event

First-aid area, where injuries can be treated

Underground delivery point

550,000 m³ (19,415,000 ft³) of soil was removed before building could begin

Into the future

Predicting the future in the Olympic Games is a difficult task. Future venues are known seven years in advance, but no-one can say for certain which athletes will compete there or who the medal winners will be. Now that the winter and summer Olympics are held in separate years, sports fans have to wait for only two years to cheer home new heroes. Millions of spectators worldwide will watch the events unfold. There will be triumphs and disasters, controversies and record-breaking performances. Whatever happens, all the athletes have to be able to cope with the extremely pressurized, competitive, and commercial environment of today's Games.

The following sports will be contested at the Athens 2004 summer Olympic Games.

AQUATICS
Diving
Swimming
Synchronized
  swimming
Water polo

ARCHERY
ATHLETICS
BADMINTON
BASEBALL
BASKETBALL
BOXING
CANOE/KAYAK
Slalom
Sprint

CYCLING
Mountain bike
Road
Track

EQUESTRIAN
Dressage
Show-jumping
Three-day event

FENCING

GYMNASTICS
Artistic
Rhythmic
Trampolining

HANDBALL
HOCKEY
JUDO
MODERN PENTATHLON
ROWING
SAILING
SHOOTING
SOCCER

WOMEN'S WRESTLING
Wrestling is the world's oldest competitive sport. There are two wrestling disciplines in the Olympic Games, Greco-Roman wrestling, where competitors use and hold only the arms or upper body, and freestyle wrestling, where the legs can also be used for pushing, lifting, and tripping. Women will compete in freestyle wrestling for the first time at the 2004 Athens Games.

Future venues

Organizing committees spend years preparing a bid for their city to host the Games. The IOC tries to ensure that the Games are spread around the world, so it does not award two consecutive Games to the same country. Since 1992, the Games have been awarded to North America, Australia, and Europe.

STARTING YOUNG
Young athletes who dream of becoming famous Olympians must be prepared for years of dedication and hard work. They also need exceptional talent and some good luck.

SUMMER SPORTS

Triathlete preparing for the cycle ride

SOFTBALL	VOLLEYBALL
TABLE TENNIS	Beach volleyball
TAEKWONDO	Volleyball
TENNIS	WEIGHT-LIFTING
TRIATHLON	WRESTLING
	Freestyle
	Greco-Roman

TRIATHLON
A new Olympic sport in Sydney was the triathlon, in which athletes have to compete in three sports, one straight after another. They swim 1.5 km (0.9 miles), cycle 40 km (25 miles), and run 10 km (6.2 miles). The first over the line wins. Any sport's international governing body can apply to be included in the Games. If the sport meets certain conditions, it can be recognized as an Olympic sport.

BEIJING 2008
The eyes of the world will be on Beijing, China, when the summer Games take place there in 2008. After seven busy years of preparation, China will host the Olympics for the first time.

TURIN 2006
The 2006 winter Games will take place in Turin, Italy. The city has constructed three Olympic villages in Turin, Bardonecchia, and Sestriere, and sports venues in seven different places. More than 2,500 athletes are expected to participate in the events, which will take place over 16 days.

PARALYMPIC SUMMER SPORTS

The following sports will be contested at the Athens 2004 Paralympic Games.

ARCHERY
ATHLETICS
BASKETBALL
BOCCIA
CYCLING
EQUESTRIAN
FENCING
GOALBALL
JUDO
POWER-LIFTING
RUGBY
SAILING
SHOOTING
SOCCER
SWIMMING
TABLE TENNIS
TENNIS
VOLLEYBALL

Rose Hill of Great Britain at Atlanta

WINTER SPORTS

The following sports will be contested at the Turin 2006 winter Games.

BIATHLON	SNOWBOARDING
BOBSLED	FREESTYLE SKIING
CURLING	NORDIC SKIING
FIGURE SKATING	NORDIC COMBINATION
ICE HOCKEY	SKI JUMPING
LUGE	
SPEED SKATING	
ALPINE SKIING	

SKELETON
Skeleton originated in the Swiss town of St Moritz in the 1800s. The name comes from the early sledges, which were thought to look like skeletons. Reintroduced as an event at the 2002 Games, skeleton involves racing down a steep run head first gripping a metal sledge.

PARALYMPIC WINTER SPORTS

The following sports will be contested at the Turin 2006 Paralympic Games.

BIATHLON	SKIING
ICE-SLEDGE HOCKEY	Alpine
	Nordic
ICE-SLEDGE RACING	

Did you know?

AMAZING FACTS

Badminton is the world's fastest racket sport, with shuttlecock speeds of 260 km (161 miles) per hour. Players need quick reflexes, but also stamina – some players have covered more than 6 km (3.7 miles) in a single match.

Ethiopian Abebe Bikila was born on the day of the 1932 Olympic marathon. Twenty-eight years later he won the Olympic marathon in Rome, running barefoot. In 1964, he won it again, but this time he wore shoes and socks.

In 1984, Nawal El Moutawakel won the 400 m hurdles, becoming the first woman from an Islamic nation and the first Moroccan to win a gold medal.

Nawal El Moutawakel wins gold

Shortly after David Douillet (France) became heavyweight judo champion at Atlanta in 1996, he was seriously injured in a motorbike accident. But he worked hard to rehabilitate himself and managed to win gold again at the Sydney Games.

Australian Ian Thorpe, called by some "the Thorpedo", was only 17 at the time of the Sydney Olympics. Yet he succeeded in swimming his way to three gold medals and one silver medal.

Ian Thorpe

In 1964, there was not enough snow at Innsbruck for the winter Games. So the Austrian army moved 20,000 ice bricks for the bobsled and luge runs, and 40,000 cubic metres (52,320 cubic yds) of snow to the Alpine skiing courses.

In medieval England, hockey was so popular that it was banned, because it was distracting people from their archery practice!

In 1952, women were able to compete in Olympic dressage for the first time. Lis Hartel (Denmark) won silver even though she was paralysed from the knees down, and had to be helped on and off her horse.

When 18-year-old Birgit Fischer from Germany won the kayak singles in 1980, she became the youngest canoeing champion in Olympic history. Twenty years later at the Sydney Games, she won two more gold medals, in the fours and in the kayak pairs, to become the only canoeist to win Olympic medals 20 years apart.

Micheline Ostermeyer (France) had amazing hands. Not only was she the 1948 women's Olympic champion at shot put and discus, but she was also a concert pianist!

The Austrian army moving snow

In 1948, 17-year-old Bob Mathias (USA) became Olympic champion in the decathlon a mere four months after he had taken up the event.

Birgit Fischer in the kayak pairs

Table tennis started in 19th-century England as an after-dinner alternative to lawn tennis, using cigar-box lids as rackets and a carved cork as a ball. It has become one of the world's largest participation sports, with 40 million competitive players worldwide.

QUESTIONS AND ANSWERS

Q Which countries have competed at all of the modern Olympic Games?

A Australia, France, Great Britain, Greece, and Switzerland are the five countries that have attended all of the Games since they began in Athens in 1896.

Q Which sports have featured at all the modern Olympic Games?

A Athletics, cycling, fencing, gymnastics, and swimming are the only five sports that have been part of every modern summer Games.

Marjorie Gestring

Q How young are competitors in the Olympic Games?

A Marjorie Gestring (USA), who became Olympic champion in springboard diving in 1936 at the age of 13 years and 9 months, is the youngest gold medallist in the summer Games, while the youngest winter gold medallist is Kim Yoon-Mi of Korea, who won the short-track speed skating in 1994 at the age of 13 years and 2 months.

Q When did curling start?

A Curling originated in Scotland in the 16th century, as a game played on frozen ponds and lochs. In the early days stones were taken from river bottoms, but later stones with handles were used. In the 20th century, people started playing on indoor ice rinks.

Q What was volleyball originally called?

A Invented in 1895 in Massachusetts, USA, volleyball was first known as "Minnonette". It quickly spread around the world, and became an Olympic sport in 1964. Beach volleyball is now hugely popular in America and Brazil.

Q When did women first compete in the Olympic Games?

A Women first took part in the second modern Games in 1900. It has always been thought that Charlotte Cooper of Great Britain became the first female individual champion when she won the tennis singles. Golf and yachting were two other sports in which women competed in 1900.

Q Why did the 1994 Lillehammer winter Games take place only two years after the 1992 Albertville Games?

A In 1986 the International Olympic Committee decided it would be better for the summer and winter Games to be in different years. In order to adjust to this new schedule, the Lillehammer Games were held in 1994 rather than in 1996.

Q When were the Olympics first shown on television?

A The 1936 Olympics were shown on screens throughout the city of Berlin, and the 1948 London Olympics were broadcast on home TV, although few people in Britain owned a television set at that time. The 1960 Rome Olympic Games were the first to be broadcast globally on television.

Q How did John Curry change men's figure skating?

A Some judges did not approve of Curry's balletic skating style because he

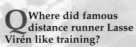

John Curry

emphasised grace and artistic expression. However, for the 1976 Games, Curry added athletic jumps to his usual style and was awarded the highest-ever points total in men's figure skating.

Q Where did famous distance runner Lasse Virén like training?

A Both in 1972 and 1976, Lasse Virén succeeded in winning the double of the 5000 m and 10,000 m. He was a strong supporter of running in woods, because constantly changing rhythm to avoid the tree roots trains you to be alert at all times, which is vital in a competition.

Q What route does the torch relay follow?

A The torch relay always starts at Olympia in Greece and travels to the city hosting the Olympics. The route is different for each Games. For the 2004 Athens Games the Olympic flame will go to each of the five continents represented by the Olympic rings before it returns to Greece.

Muhammad Ali lighting the cauldron at the 1996 Atlanta Games

Record Breakers

🏆 USA has won over 2,300 summer medals, more than any other country.

🏆 Norway has won 263 winter medals, more than any other country.

🏆 The oldest Olympic champion is Oscar Swahn (Sweden), who won gold in shooting in 1912, when he was 64. Eight years later, he won silver at the age of 72.

🏆 The oldest female Olympic champion is Queenie Newall (Great Britain), who won gold in archery in 1908, at the age of 53.

🏆 More people were involved in the Sydney Olympics than in any other Games. Over 10,000 athletes took part, in 300 events, representing 200 countries. In the 1896 Athens Games, there were only 14 countries, 211 athletes, and 43 events.

Sydney Olympic Stadium

Famous Olympians

MANY OLYMPIC ATHLETES become famous all over the world. Some are well known because they have won a number of medals, others because they have broken records, or are the first to achieve a particular feat. They may capture the public imagination with a stunning performance in the gym, on the ice rink, or on the slopes. All have to be single-minded and determined as they follow arduous, long-term training and competition programmes in preparation for the Games.

BJÖRN DÆHLIE
NORWAY, SKIING, BORN 19 JUNE 1967, 8 GOLD, 4 SILVER
Before he was even ten years old, Björn Dæhlie went on long cross-country ski trips with his father. He developed into the greatest cross-country skier in history, becoming Olympic champion eight times.

TOMAS GUSTAFSON
SWEDEN, SKATING, BORN 28 DECEMBER 1959, 3 GOLD, 1 SILVER
In 1984, Tomas Gustafson became champion in the 5000 m speed skating by the narrow margin of one-fiftieth of a second, but lost the 10,000 m by one-twentieth of a second.

Tomas Gustafson

SUMMER OLYMPICS

NIKOLAY ANDRIANOV
USSR, GYMNASTICS, BORN 14 OCTOBER 1952, 7 GOLD, 5 SILVER, 3 BRONZE
At the 1976 Montreal Games, Andrianov dominated men's gymnastics in an unprecedented way, winning four gold medals, one silver, one bronze, and a team silver. Over his career he won more medals than any other male competitor.

KRISZTINA EGERSZEGI
HUNGARY, AQUATICS, BORN 16 AUGUST 1974, 5 GOLD, 1 SILVER, 1 BRONZE
Egerszegi was only 14 years old when she competed in the 1988 Games. Even though she weighed only 45 kg (7 st) she won a silver in the 100 m and a gold in the 200 m backstroke. She went on to win a total of five individual event gold medals.

CATHY FREEMAN
AUSTRALIA, ATHLETICS, BORN 16 FEBRUARY 1973, 1 GOLD, 1 SILVER
In 1996, Cathy Freeman won silver in the 400 m, becoming the first Aborigine to win an Olympic medal. Chosen to light the cauldron at the opening ceremony for the Sydney Games, Freeman personified Australia's hope for the Games. Wearing her special suit, she went on to win gold in the 400 m.

HAILE GEBRSELASSIE
ETHIOPIA, ATHLETICS, BORN 18 APRIL 1973, 2 GOLD
As a child in Ethiopia, Haile Gebrselassie ran 10 km (6 miles) to school each day, and 10 km (6 miles) back again. When he first started training as an adult, he used to run with his left arm crooked, where his schoolbooks had been. He has won gold twice in the 10,000 m, winning each race with a sprint finish.

ALADAR GEREVICH
HUNGARY, FENCING, BORN 16 MARCH 1910, DIED 14 MAY 1991, 7 GOLD, 1 SILVER, 2 BRONZE
Between 1932 and 1960, Aladar Gerevich won six successive gold medals in the sabre team event, setting a record for any Olympic sport. The world's greatest sabreur, he also won gold, silver, and bronze in the individual sabre competitions.

STEFFI GRAF
GERMANY, TENNIS, BORN 14 JUNE 1969, 1 GOLD, 1 SILVER, 1 BRONZE
In 1984, 15-year-old Steffi Graf won the Olympic tennis demonstration tournament although she was the youngest contestant. In 1988, she won the Australian Open, the French Open, Wimbledon, the US Open, and the Olympic title, achieving the first ever "Golden Slam". She was awarded the Olympic Order in 1999.

Michael Johnson

Steffi Graf

MICHAEL JOHNSON
USA, ATHLETICS, BORN 13 SEPTEMBER 1967, 5 GOLD
At the 1996 Games, Michael Johnson became Olympic champion at 200 m and 400 m, winning both finals by a big margin.

OLGA KORBUT
RUSSIA, GYMNASTICS, BORN 16 MAY 1955, 4 GOLD, 2 SILVER MEDALS
Seventeen-year-old Olga Korbut charmed the public at the Munich Olympics in 1972. One day she caused a sensation with her spectacular routine on the uneven parallel bars, two days later she committed three errors and wept. Korbut

Cathy Freeman

WINTER OLYMPICS

In 1988, he won both, setting a new world record in the 10,000 m, which he won by almost eight seconds.

VONETTA FLOWERS
USA, BOBSLED, BORN 29 OCTOBER 1973, 1 GOLD
In 2002 at the Salt Lake City Games, Vonetta Flowers won gold in the bobsled, becoming the first African American champion in the winter Olympics. A former track and field athlete, she switched to bobsled after failing to qualify for the 1996 and 2000 summer Olympics.

GEORG HACKL
GERMANY, LUGE, BORN 9 SEPTEMBER 1966, 3 GOLD, 2 SILVER

Vonetta Flowers

Georg Hackl has won medals in singles luge at five consecutive Olympics. He was champion in 1992, 1994, and 1998, and won silver in 1988 and 2002.

KJETIL ANDRE AAMODT
NORWAY, SKIING, BORN 2 SEPTEMBER 1971, 3 GOLD, 2 SILVER, 2 BRONZE
Three months before the 1992 Games, Kjetil Andre Aamodt was extremely ill. He lost 11 kg (24 lbs) and was only able to return to training six weeks before the Games, and yet he went on to win his first gold. He was a great all-round Alpine skier, winning medals in super G, giant slalom, downhill, and combined.

LYDIA SKOBLIKOVA
RUSSIA, SKATING, BORN 8 MARCH 1939, 6 GOLD

At the 1960 Games Lydia Skoblikova was Olympic champion at two different skating distances. In 1964, she became the first person to gain four gold medals at one winter Games, winning the 500 m, the 1000 m, the 1500 m, and the 3000 m.

Georg Hackl

MARJA-LIISA KIRVESNIEMI-HÄMÄLÄINEN
FINLAND, SKIING, BORN 10 SEPTEMBER 1955, 3 GOLD, 4 BRONZE
Kirvesniemi-Hämäläinen competed in six winter Olympics. In 1984, she easily won all three women's cross-country events. In 1994, at the age of 38, she won bronze in both the 5-km and the 30-km races.

---

later received so much fan mail that the post office had to get an extra member of staff to sort her mail alone!

LARISSA LATYNINA
RUSSIAN FEDERATION, BORN 20 DECEMBER 1934, 9 GOLD, 5 SILVER, 4 BRONZE
Between 1956 and 1964 gymnast Larissa Latynina won 18 medals, more than any other athlete. After her retirement she became the national gymnastics team coach.

ELISABETA LIPA-OLENIUC
ROMANIA, BORN 26 OCTOBER 1964, 4 GOLD, 2 SILVER, 1 BRONZE
Lipa-Oleniuc started with a gold and a silver in the double sculls, gained a gold in the single sculls, a bronze in the quadruple sculls, and finally two golds in the coxed eights. She has won more Olympic medals than any other rower.

VALENTYN MANKIN
RUSSIAN FEDERATION, SAILING, BORN 19 AUGUST 1938, 3 GOLD, 1 SILVER
In 1968, Mankin stormed to victory in the Finn class. In 1972, he switched to the Tempest class and won that. At the 1980 Moscow Games, Mankin switched again and narrowly won the Star class. He is the only sailor in Olympic history to win gold medals in three different classes.

MARIE-JOSÉ PÉREC
FRANCE, BORN 9 MAY 1968, 3 GOLD
Born on the island of Guadeloupe, Marie-José Pérec moved to Paris when she was 16 years old and became the most successful female French athlete of all time.

Haile Gebrselassie

In 1992, she won the 400 m but at the 1996 Atlanta Games she won both the 200 m and the 400 m.

FÉLIX SAVON
CUBA, BOXING, BORN 22 SEPTEMBER 1967, 3 GOLD
Félix Savon dominated heavyweight boxing from 1986 onwards, but Cuba boycotted the 1988 Seoul Games, so Savon did not become

Olympic champion until 1992. He retained the title in 1996 and again at Sydney in 2000.

SOO-NYUNG KIM
KOREA, ARCHERY, BORN 5 APRIL 1971, 4 GOLD, 1 SILVER, 1 BRONZE
Nicknamed the "Viper", Soo-Nyung Kim dominated archery during the 1990s, holding the women's world records for all distances.

KAROLY TAKACS
HUNGARY, SHOOTING, BORN 21 JANUARY 1910, DIED 5 JANUARY 1976, 2 GOLD
In 1938, Takacs was serving in the army when a grenade shattered his right hand. A member of the Hungarian pistol-shooting team, Takacs taught himself to shoot with his left hand, and went on to win two gold medals for rapid-fire pistol shooting.

Soo-Nyung Kim

Find out more

THERE ARE MANY WAYS of finding out more about the Olympic Games. The cities hosting the next summer and winter Olympics will be hard at work preparing for the event and publicising what is going to happen. Looking further ahead, other cities will be putting forward bids to host future Olympics. Through your national Olympic Association you can find out the dates and methods for selecting your country's teams, and also information about the training and support the athletes receive.

torino 2006

OLYMPICS AND CULTURE
Turin is organizing a programme of artistic and cultural events to take place alongside the Olympic winter Games in February 2006.

Construction work in Athens for the 2004 Games

USEFUL WEBSITES

- The official website of the Olympic Movement is: **www.olympic.org**. It has sections on sports, past Games, famous athletes, and the structure of the Olympic Movement.
- For information about the Olympic Museum and Study Centre, Lausanne, Switzerland, see: **www.olympic.org/uk/passion/index_uk.asp**
- To find out about the Olympic Games to be held in Athens, Turin and Beijing see: **www.olympic.org/uk/games/athens/index_uk.asp** **www.torino2006.org/eng/index.asp** **www.beijing_2008.org**
- To find out more about the Paralympics, go to: **www.paralympic.org**

THE OLYMPIC MUSEUM
A visit to the Olympic Museum and Studies Centre in Switzerland will immerse you in the history of the Olympics. Audio-visual shows, 3D presentations, and interactive terminals recreate the intense, exciting atmosphere of the Games. The Museum also has extensive collections of Olympic items, such as torches and medals, and objects that belonged to famous Olympians, such as Jean-Claude Killy's skis and boots.

ATHENS 2004
Building up-to-date facilities for all the sports together with accommodation for all the athletes in the Olympic village is a huge task. Architects, planners, and builders have to work together, to ensure that everything is ready on time. Transport facilities must also be able to cope with the huge influx of visitors for the Games.

A model of Olympic facilities at Athens

Places to visit

THE OLYMPIC MUSEUM AND STUDIES CENTRE, LAUSANNE, SWITZERLAND
Opened in June 1993, the Museum has the following permanent exhibitions:
• The Olympic Adventure, chronicling the history and origins of the Olympic Movement.
• The Athletes and the Games, dedicated to the athletes who have left their mark on the Games.
There are guided, thematic visits, with films, demonstrations, and the chance to handle objects, on the following topics:
• The Games of Antiquity
• The Olympic flame and torch relay
• The path of an Olympic Champion
• Art and the Olympic Movement

The Olympic Studies Centre has an archive section, a library, and an education service. There is also a picture and sound department with more than 18,200 hours of film footage, and a photographic library.

OLYMPIA, GREECE
The site of the ancient Olympic Games, where the torch is lit at the start of each Olympiad.

Gold medal from the 1960 Rome Games

THE PANATHENEAN STADIUM, ATHENS, GREECE
A replica of an ancient Greek stadium, built for the 1896 Games. It is long and thin and constructed out of white marble.

JOIN THE RACE
If there is a sport that interests you, investigate local clubs and competitive events. These young athletes are taking part in the London Heathrow Youth Games, an annual competition covering 29 different sports for Londoners between eleven and 19 years of age.

Olympic rings and wreath

THE OLYMPIC FLAME
Find out the route for the next torch relay and go and see it if you can. The torch relay acts as a call to bring together the world's athletes for the Games. Lit at Olympia in Greece, the torch relay for Athens will visit at least 27 cities around the world before touring Greece and returning to Athens for the opening ceremony.

The torch for the Athens Games

VOLUNTEERS SAVE THE DAY
Thousands of volunteers helped the Sydney Games to run smoothly. Some worked at the venues, others on transport, but many simply helped visitors to find their way from one place to another. Future Games will also need a large number of helpers to ensure the event goes well.

Sydney volunteers agreed to work a minimum of ten eight-hour shifts, but some ended up doing more than 20 shifts

Glossary

Discus

ALPINE SKIING Skiing events, such as slalom and downhill, held on steep prepared slopes.

AMATEUR Someone who takes part in a sport or other activity for pleasure rather than profit.

AMPHORA Greek or Roman two-handled narrow-necked jar for oil.

AQUATICS The four Olympic sports that take place in a swimming pool: swimming, diving, synchronised swimming, and water polo.

ARCHAEOLOGISTS People who study the past by analysing cultural remains.

ATHLETE A person who has trained to compete in a sport.

ATHLETICS Events that take place on the track and the field. There are running, hurdling, throwing, and jumping events.

BIATHLON A contest in which skiers with rifles shoot at targets on a cross-country course.

BINDINGS The mechanisms on downhill skis that release the skis when you fall over, but stop them from sliding away.

BOBSLED A race for two or four people, who sit in a sledge and go down a steep, twisting, ice-covered run.

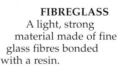

Kamila Skolimowska (Poland), who won gold in the women's hammer at the 2000 Sydney Games

BOYCOTT To refuse to have anything to do with a person or event.

COMBAT SPORTS There are five Olympic sports that involve combat: boxing, fencing, judo, taekwondo, and wrestling.

CYCLING The Olympic sports involving bicycles are track racing, road racing, mountain biking, and triathlon.

DECATHLON An athletic contest for men in which each athlete competes in ten different events: 100 m, long jump, shot put, high jump, 400 m, 110 m hurdles, discus, pole vault, javelin, and 1500 m

DEHYDRATION The loss of water from the body tissues. Athletes have to take care that they do not become dehydrated.

DRUG TESTS Tests that athletes undergo to check for substances they might be using to improve their performance.

EQUESTRIAN SPORTS There are four events involving horses: show-jumping, dressage, the three-day event, and the modern pentathlon.

EVENT One contest within the programme of contests for a particular sport.

FIBREGLASS A light, strong material made of fine glass fibres bonded with a resin.

FITNESS Being in good health and well prepared for an event.

GYMNASIUM A hall with bars, weights, and ropes for physical training.

GYMNASTICS The sports that take place in a gymnasium and demonstrate strength and agility. The three Olympic events are artistic gymnastics, rhythmic gymnastics, and trampolining.

HEPTATHLON An athletic contest for women. Each athlete competes in seven events: 100 m hurdles, high jump, shot put, 200 m, long jump, javelin, and 800 m.

INDIVIDUAL EVENTS Events in which individuals compete on their own.

INTERCALATED GAMES The Games celebrated in 1906, ten years after the first modern Games. They were inserted in the middle of the Olympiad between the 1904 and the 1908 Games.

Ice hockey on a Russian stamp for the 1960 winter Games

INTERNATIONAL OLYMPIC COMMITTEE The international body in charge of the Olympic Games. The committee decides where to hold the Games and which sports to include.

LOGO Several letters, or a symbol, used to represent something else. The Olympic logo is used a lot in advertising for the Games and on souvenirs sold to the vast numbers of visitors who come to watch the Games.

LUGE A race in which the competitors lie back on a lightweight toboggan and go feet-first down a steep, twisting, ice-covered run.

MARATHON A race on foot that is 42.195 km (26 miles, 385 yds) long.

MODERN PENTATHLON A contest in which each competitor takes part in five different sports. The sports are: riding, épée fencing, swimming, pistol shooting, and running. In the Ancient Games pentathlon athletes had to run, jump, throw the discus and javelin, and wrestle.

NORDIC SKIING Cross-country skiing, ski jumping, and biathlon.

OLIVE WREATH A band of olive leaves awarded to the winner as an honour at the ancient Olympic Games.

OLYMPIA The religious sanctuary where the Ancient Olympic Games were held.

OLYMPIAD The four-year period between one Olympic Games and the next.

OLYMPIC FLAG The flag bearing the five Olympic rings.

OLYMPIC OATH An oath made on behalf of competitors to compete in accordance with the rules and in a spirit of sportsmanship. There is also an oath made on behalf of the officials.

OLYMPIC RINGS The five linked rings that represent Africa, Asia, America, Europe, and Australasia, the five continents that take part in the Games.

OLYMPIC VILLAGE Accommodation built to house all the competitors taking part in the Games.

OPENING CEREMONY A display to mark the opening of the Games.

PANATHENEAN STADIUM An ancient stadium rebuilt for the first modern Olympic Games in Athens.

PANHELLENIC GAMES The Pythian, Nemean, Isthmian, and Olympic Games, the four national festivals in Ancient Greece.

PARALYMPICS A sporting event, modelled on the Olympic Games, held for disabled competitors.

PROFESSIONAL Someone who takes part in a sport or other activity in order to make money.

PUCK The small disc of hard rubber used in ice hockey.

PURSUIT RACING A cycling race in which the riders start on

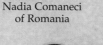

Nadia Comaneci of Romania

opposite sides of the track and try to overtake their opponents.

RACQUET AND BAT SPORTS The Olympic sports in this category are tennis, table tennis, badminton, baseball, and softball.

SKATING The two skating sports are figure skating and speed skating.

SKELETON A race on a very light toboggan down a steep, twisting, ice-covered run. Competitors go down the run head first.

SNOWBOARDING An alpine sport in which competitors slide across the snow on a shaped board. Halfpipe and slalom are Olympic events in snowboarding.

SPONSORS Companies that give athletes or competition organisers money so that they will advertise the company's products.

SPORT A type of athletic activity, with a specific structure and rules.

SPORTSMANSHIP Competing fairly in a competition, according to the rules in force, and maintaining good humour if losing.

STADIUM A sports arena with facilities for spectators.

STREAMLINING Making sure that the shape of your body or the vehicle that you are using offers the minimum resistance to the air or water around it.

TARGET SPORTS The Olympic sports that involve aiming at an object are archery, shooting, and biathlon.

TEAM EVENTS Events such as a relay race, in which members of a team run one after the other. Also events such as dressage, in which team members' scores or times are totalled.

TEAM SPORTS Sports such as football or ice hockey, where members of one team compete together against members of an opposing team.

TECHNIQUE Proficiency in a particular practical skill.

A shoe with spikes for track-and-field competition

TORCH RELAY The carrying of the flame, mainly by runners, from Olympia, Greece, to the stadium in the city hosting the Games.

TRIATHLON A contest in which each competitor takes part in three different sports: swimming, cycling, and running.

VOLUNTEERS People who give their time and energy to help competitors and tourists who come to the Olympic Games.

WATER SPORTS There are four Olympic outdoor sports that take place on water: canoeing, kayaking, rowing, and sailing.

WEIGHT-LIFTING There are two events in weight-lifting: the clean and jerk, and the snatch.

WEIGHT TRAINING Physical exercises which involve lifting weights in order to improve muscle performance.

Chris Boardman (Great Britain) on his pursuit track bicycle

Eyewitness titles in this series:

Future titles to include:

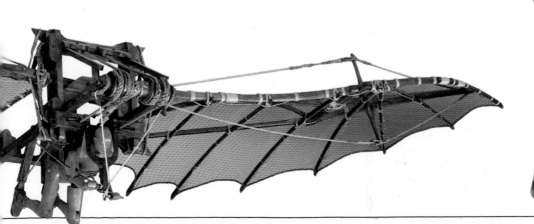

Index

Acknowledgements

Dorling Kindersley would like to thank:

Athletes Robert Earwicker (weight-lifter), Rose Hill (Paralympian), Kathy Read (swimmer), Anthony Sawyer (decathlete); Mary Sharman (dressage rider)

Model maker Paul Fowler

Nutritionist Jane Griffin (Consultant nutritionist to the British Olympic Association)

Designers of the Sydney Olympic Stadium Bligh Lobb Sports Architecture

Index: Chris Bernstein

The publishers would also like to thank the following for their kind permission to reproduce their photographs:

Position Key: a=above: b=below; c=centre; l=left; r=right; t=top

Action Plus: Chris Barry 27tr; Glyn Kirk 27br, 48bl, 55tr; Neil Tingle 26br, 42bl; Peter Sourrier 34tl; Tony Henshaw 33br; Richard Francis 65tl.

AKG London: 14bc; Erich Lessing 9tr; John Hios 12bc, 13bc, 14tr, 14cr, 15cr; Musée du Louvre, Paris 30c; Olympia Museum 30cr;
alamy.com: Ethel Davies/Imagestate 59bc; 64-65.
Allsport: 17bc, 20cr, 21tl, 32cl, 33tl, 33bl, 34cl, 56cl; Agence Vandystadt/Bruno Bade 23br; Clive Brunskill 27tl, 27bl; Gary M Prior 17tr; Gray Mortimore 29tr, 29tl, 29tc, 29cr; Hulton Getty 19cr; IOC/Olympic Museum Collections 4l, 5bc, 6tl, 15br, 15tl, 16tr, 16bc, 16br, 17crr, 17cr, 17c, 17cl, 17cll, 17crrr, 17tl, 17bl, 18c, 18tr, 19tl, 19bl, 20tl, 22cl, 25tl, 34crb, 44c, 44b, 44-45t, 45b, 46ac, 46c, 46bc, 47br, 47bc, 47tr, 52tr, 52bl, 53bl, 55br, 55tl; John Gichigi 37tc; Michael Cooper 37tr; Mike Hewitt 22tr; Mike Powell 22br, 37cr, 47tc, 58cl; Nick Wilson 54cr; Pascal Rondeau 23tc, 26-27c; Shaun Botterill 26tr, 39tr; Simon Bruty 23cr, 26bl; SOCOG 21tr; Stephen Dunn 54br; Stu Forster 59br; Todd Warshaw 29bl; Tony Duffy 21br, 21cl;
Ancient Art & Architecture Collection: 8c, 11cr, 11bl, 13br, 13l, 16bl;
Associated Press: 54bl; Dimitri Messinis 64c;
Athens 2004 Olympic Games Organising Committee: 65tc.

British Museum, London: 8bl, 9br, 10r, 10tl, 11tl, 11br, 16tl, 30-31b, 32tl, 43tr;
Colorsport: 31crb, 56cra, 58bl, 59tl; Andy Cowie 63br;
Corbis UK Ltd: 31cra; Bettmann 61cl, Seguin Franck/Corbis Sygma 65bc, James Marshall 61br, Prevosto Olivier/Corbis Sygma 66bc, Chris Trotman 63cal;
Deutsches Archäologisches Institut, Berlin: 12c;
Empics Ltd: Aubrey Washington 24bl, 31br; DPA 62-63, Tony Marshall 59br; 62bcl; 63clb; 66-67; 68-69, S/ALPHA 60cl, Uwe Speck 63tr, Witters 61tr; 62br;
E.T. Archive: 12tl, 18cl;
Mary Evans Picture Library: 10cl, 30tr;
Getty Images: Doug Armand 58-58b, David Cannon 67bl, Tony Duffy 67tc, Tony Feder 65ccl, Chris Hondros 64cl, I.O.C. 34br; 65cr, Jed Jacobsohn 58cl, Gray Mortimore 62tc, Adam Pretty 60b, Pascal Rondeau 62c;
Sonia Halliday Photographs: 8tr, 50cr;
Michael Holford: 10bl, 13tr;
Hulton Getty: 50tl, 53cr, 60tr;
Imperial War Museum: 52c;
IOC/Olympic Museum Collections: 15bl, 25bl, 32bl, 33tr, 35tl, 43tc, 43c, 46-47tc, 50br, 51tl, 53br; Claude Bornand 64bc;

The Kobal Collection: Olympia-Film 32tr, 34bc, 35cr;
Pa Photos: EPA European Press Agency 60cr
Popperfoto: 15tr, 20tc, 25c, 32br, 33bc, 34tr, 35bc, 52cr, 53t; Dave Joiner 25bc, 25abc;
Rex Features: Sipa Press 53cl, 54tr; Roger-Viollet 12bl, 12br, 14br; Andrew Murray 60-61, Sporting Pictures (UK) Ltd (SPP) 61cb;
Scala: Museo della Terme, Roma 9l;
Science Photo Library: David Ducros 55cr; Philippe Plailly/Eurelios 36bl;
Seiko Europe Ltd: 50bl, 50cl, 51br, 51bc, 51cra, 51tr;
Sporting Pictures (UK) Ltd: 35c;
Tony Stone Images: Chuck Pefley 58br; George Grigoriou 59bl;
Topham Picturepoint: 55bl.
Torino Organising Committee XX Olympic Winter Games: 64tl.
All other images © Dorling Kindersley
For further information see:
www.dkimages.com